Contents

Calla Press

where broken storytellers tell the holy story

Spring Literary Journal 2025 | Living in Wonder

BY ARTIST *Caroline Greb*

CALLA PRESS
PUBLISHING

Spring 2025, Editor-in-Chief: Rosa Gilbert
Compiled by Caitlin Callahan, Spring Intern
Cover Artist: Caroline Greb

ISBN: 978-1-966828-06-8

Letter from the Editor

Dear Calla Press community,

I've been pondering the desert-roaming Israelites a lot lately. Mainly, because I feel so similar to them most of the time. Grumbling. Struggling with discontentment. Lacking wonder at the myriad ways in which God provides for me. It was with them (and myself) in mind that the theme for this journal came to be.

Ever since we announced the theme, my prayer for this journal has been that contributors and readers alike would be encouraged to seek the wonder of Christ in their everyday lives—no matter what circumstances or "deserts" they might be walking through. As I read each submission that was sent in, my heart was uplifted, blessed, and spurred on in my walk with the Lord. I know it will be so for all who read it as well.

To our contributors: thank you for embracing this call to live in wonder and for so beautifully putting it into words. Each of your pieces is so unique, but each points back to this truth: we can indeed taste and see that the Lord is good when we live in constant wonder of who He is and what He does for us. Thank you for trusting us with your work.

To our readers: be blessed as you flip through these pages. Be reminded of the Lord's goodness. Be encouraged to praise Him and thank Him for all the small ways in which He shows us that He loves and cares for us.

May this journal be a fountain of truth that you can come back to again and again whenever you find yourself lacking faith in the desert. May it renew your sense of wonder with each reading.

Enjoy,
Rosa Gilbert, Editor-in-Chief

Letter from the Compiler

Do you live in a daily, moment-by-moment sense of wonder?
I should.
But I don't.
Because my eyes are constantly fixed on a crick in my lower neck, a due-tomorrow marketing quiz, a sedan that just cut me off in traffic.

Yes, some of these things are worth looking at. Some of them? We may glance at—for a second.

But what should we *fix* our eyes on? A better question: to *whom*? We know the verse. We know the song.

As we go about our moment-by-moment struggles, temptations, complications, to whom do we fix our eyes? Because if we're fixing our eyes on the world, we'll end up complaining about the pain, fearing the quiz, yelling at the "sedan." But when we fix our eyes heavenward—which can mean downward, to the Word—we thank God that we have necks in the first place; we cast our cares on the God who can quiet our minds; we ask God for otherworldly strength to love others, even our enemies.

We see the moment-by-moment as a call to honor the Creator and glory in His creation and love. We smile at rainbows, God's promise to mankind. We cover our mouths, tears rushing from our eyelids, as we ask God for mercy and help, crying out as David in Psalm 70. When we live in Christ, we learn to live in wonder: and if not at the world, at the Lord of it.

And so, dear reader, I hope that these poems, short stories, and fiction pieces do to you as many of them have done to me: yes—leave you in awe-filled tears—but also unveil the beauty of the everyday through an eternal, holy lens.

Because that's what living in wonder is about. Not necessarily altering the circumstances. But shifting the perspective. Shifting our eyes to Jesus, "the author and finisher of our faith."

—Caitlin Callahan, Spring 2025 Intern

Featured Work

A note to our contributors and readers: We received many *wonderful* submissions to this journal. It seems that many of you resonated with this theme, and your words shone as a result. Due to the numerous incredible pieces, we have decided to highlight a select few. In the following pages, you'll find several poems and essays that we felt best expressed what it means to *live in wonder.* However, we want to be clear that all the pieces published in this journal are a blessing and will truly convince any reader that *Living in Wonder* of God and his creation is the best way to live!

Roam the Blessed Earth

By Kris Ann Valdez

Since the days of Moses, we have not outlived trees
nor since Elijah has a fire-enshrouded chariot flown—
But yesterday, 5000 dolphins stampeded off the California coast
an octopus starved herself so that her young might live
and a single oyster filtered 50 gallons of pollutants from the ocean
Such wonders.

The God of Moses and Elijah—
isn't he also the God of dolphins, oysters, and octopi?
That God gave the giraffe an evening song,
the hummingbird backwards flight,
slugs 4 noses, and snails 14,000 teeth
No small wonders.

An orangutan heals a nasty wound with the paste
of the Akur Kuning plant
elephants and crows perform death rituals for their deceased
and pigeons—those rats of the air—recognize human faces
nurse their young, solve math problems
Ah, what wonders.

This earth, day by day
grows older and younger in the hands of its offspring
which crawl and slither,
pulse and breathe,
jump and leap,
cry and laugh,
run and skip,
trot and prance

their way over a land subdued,
a dominion, a wonder.

Let them lift their voices, smell their smells
sense predators, friends too.
Isn't this a wonder to rival wonders of old?
That the world goes on spinning 1000 miles per hour,
unfelt
and an acorn holds the DNA to a 1000-year-old tree,
unseen.

There is feather and skin, gill and lung—
There are songs in the sky
woven through meadows,
forests, prairies, swimming
in the seven seas
stories of a 1000 generations
that roamed this blessed earth
All of it—a wonder.

The Underestimated Wonder of a Quiet Life

By Hannah Grace Staton

This is for you, dazzled dreamer whose golden sunrise dreams have faded to murky November gray; valiant visionary whose steel bravery has withered into faceless fear; gracious guide who longed to crest the mountain peak but instead slogs through the marshy plain.

Once you dreamed of greatness and glory and grandeur: feeding the hungry, freeing the prisoners, and reaching the masses. You yearned for miracles: seeing the sick healed, lost ones found, prodigals return, mountains move, walls crumble, and waters part. You longed to hear God's voice loudest of all, like crashing waves and rumbling thunder and a lion's roar.

But you open your eyes to a much different scene. You're surrounded by the small and humble and ordinary: stacks of dirty dishes piled high, little fingers clinging to your ankles, mounds of unopened envelopes and paperwork littering the kitchen table. Your prayers are mostly the two-word variety: "Lord, help!" Dust speckles the cover of your Bible, and you don't remember what you read as well as you used to. On Sunday morning, your mind is so foggy that only fragments of the sermon burrow their way into your subconscious. All week long, your ears are ringing with children's questions and clanging silverware and your phone's all-too-familiar chime, and you crave five minutes of uninterrupted silence.

And the question never leaves you: *is there beauty to be found even here?*

Hungry for Wonder

Deep inside you lies a hunger you fear to admit but dare not deny: a hunger for wonder. The distance between the life you wanted and the life you've been given stirs a longing for something more.

But what if I told you that it isn't as far away as you might think—that there's a certain kind of beauty, a certain kind of wonder, tucked inside the edges of the life you have? What if I told you that a quiet life is a gift?

Listen to what God tells us in his word: "Now concerning brotherly love you have no need for anyone to write to you, for you yourselves have been taught by God to love one another, for that indeed is what you are doing to all the brothers throughout Macedonia. But we urge you, brothers, to do this more and more, and *to aspire to live quietly*, and to mind your own affairs, and to work with your hands, as we instructed you, so that you may walk properly before outsiders and be dependent on no one" (1 Thess. 4:9–12 ESV, emphasis added).

Aspire to live a quiet life. I dare say that's not the kind of life most of us aspire to, yet that's the kind of life God calls us to lead. Why?

God's commands are for our ultimate good. He knows what is best for us, and his commands pave the path of his will.

So what is the goodness that this command guides us toward?

I believe it leads us into a life of *trust* and *rest*: trusting that God's plan will be accomplished in and through us and resting in the truth that we don't have to do it all. God doesn't command us to try to change the world all on our own; instead, he wants us to be faithful where he has placed us.

This perspective frees us to find wonder in our quiet lives, believing that a quiet life is a beautiful gift. The wonder of a quiet life is found in seeing God's fingerprints in the little things and sharing that delight with others.

Come and see.

Finding Wonder

There is such beauty and joy to be found in the little things we often take for granted. God makes his presence felt in a multitude of little ways. When you walk through life with your eyes open, you see so many beautiful things along the way.

The simplest things can bring the sweetest pleasure. Something doesn't have to be fancy or complicated to bring delight. It doesn't have to cost money. The only price it requires is your attention.

Simple things make me happy. And I'm not ashamed of that.

Things like watching calves frolic in a pasture, seeing fireflies light up the night, listening to crickets, hearing the smile in a friend's voice over the phone, the rhythmic clatter of keys when words are coming fast, the soothing sound of flowing piano notes, the sheer emotion of epic instrumentals, the light scent of lavender, a drink of water after coming in from a walk, a bowl of cheese-laced chili on a wintry night, the sun's warmth stealing in through the windows, the cozy comfort of a snuggly sweater. reading a well-loved book, and writing in my journal by lamplight. Those are all simple things, but they're special to me. And I'm sure you could make a similar list of little things that are special to you.

Even though all those joys are there, you have to look for them. Even though they're small, you have to make space for them. You can be in such a rush and frenzy that you miss what's in front of you.

It's not just the hurry of your pace that blinds your eyes; it's the hurry of your heart. Hurrying boards up the windows of your soul, causing you to rush by many lovely things without ever noticing. If you do happen to notice, your sense of urgency clams up any sense of wonder you could experience. There just isn't time to spend on little things that aren't on your list. Even if there were, what would it matter?

More than you'll ever know.

> We need Jesus to touch us. We need the Spirit to awaken us. We notice our lack of attention, we repent of our hurry, we pray for the attentive awakening touch of Christ, and we pray to be drawn into a life of love: a life of attention to God and neighbor.
>
> What will you do with your one, limited life? What will you do with your limited time? Will you dare to pay attention?[1]

---

1 Ashley Hales, *A Spacious Life* (Downers Grove, Illinois: InterVarsity Press, 2021), 75.

Just as God doesn't call us to a loud life, he doesn't call us to a speedy life. Faster isn't always better. Sometimes, for the sake of your soul, you need to slow down. When you do, you will realize how much you've been missing.

Life is luscious, like a juicy peach picked straight from the tree, its sweet and sticky juices dripping down your chin as you bite into it. But you have to take it from the tree.

Life is filled with little luxuries that cost nothing, and no man need be a beggar who has learned the secret of finding joy wherever he is. The secret lies in contentment and attentiveness.

Contentment makes you satisfied with where you are and what you have. Rather than striving for more, you're seeking to make the best use of what God has given you and serve faithfully where he has placed you. You're not looking to be somewhere else.

When you're not looking to be somewhere else, your eyes are opened to the beauty where you are. You become attentive to your surroundings, so you see things others don't. They might fancy you a starry-eyed dreamer, but the truth is they're the ones with eyes fixed on the clouds, while you're the one with both feet planted on the ground. Just because it's invisible to them doesn't mean it isn't there. Your faith enables you to recognize the richness of the soil in which you are rooted, which is why you can grow in the midst of circumstances others would find unfruitful.

Slowing to see strengthens the soul. Awaiting the art awakens the heart. Bringing forth beauty blossoms the bearer.

> You may feel broken, imperfect. You may wonder whether you are inventive enough. You may wonder whether the words you write—or the meals you make, or the portraits you paint, or the sketches you animate, or the rooms you design, or the sermons you speak, or the casting calls you get called to—are of any weight. You may wonder if any of it is worth it.
>
> But you have seen the light, and you can be the light.
>
> By way of creating, you are bringing forth light.
>
> By way of making, you are making God known.[2]

---

2 Rachel Marie Kang, *Let There Be Art* (Grand Rapids: Revell, 2022), 219.

Bearer of Wonder

As you are blessed, you're equipped to become a blessing. Out of the abundance of your own bounty pour forth streams that will water others. "Whoever brings blessing will be enriched, and one who waters will himself be watered" (Prov. 11:25 ESV).

You don't have to be loud to bless others. You can bless them in quiet ways, by doing little things that might not draw much attention or applause: a note, a call, a caring question, a listening ear, a warm meal, or a comforting hug. Even if it seems small to you, it can mean the world to someone else. Little acts of kindness can be huge gifts of joy to the recipients.

"We become great when we genuinely, happily serve in unacknowledged ways and places because that is where we find the sustaining face of God, especially when no one else sees us or applauds. Hearts that grow in God, that reach for Him and receive His reaching back, become profoundly great. Unshakable, even."[3]

Sometimes thoughtfulness is found not in what you do, but in what you don't do. Kindness doesn't always call you to come forward; sometimes it summons you to step back.

Something happened to me at the library one time that shows this. As I stood in front of the drop box stuffing my holds into the return slot, a man and his young son passed by on their way into the library. As they came back out, the father told the boy, "There's the book return."

I stepped back to let the boy go ahead and watched, smiling, as he stood on his tiptoes and slid in a few picture books.

The man nodded at me and said, "Thank you." I smiled and nodded in return. Then they left as I resumed returning my books.

It was only a small gesture of thoughtfulness, and all I had to do in order to make it happen was step back. It might not seem like much, but it meant something to me because it was proof that I don't need to be bold and flashy in order to show kindness to others—I can show genuine care in my own quiet ways. The same is true for you.

---

3 Sara Hagerty, *Unseen* (Grand Rapids: Zondervan, 2017), 68.

But just like with seeing the beauty in ordinary things, you won't discover opportunities to help others if you aren't looking. It's easy to slide into selfishness, but kindness is a choice. You have to make time for it. If you're too busy, too rushed, and too caught up in your own little world, you'll miss countless chances to give the gift of kindness.

Leave space for glimpses of wonder and acts of kindness, because these are the little things that tie our lives together.

***

This is the beauty of a quiet life. When your eyes aren't dazzled by the flashy mirrors all around you, you can see through windows of wonder into others' eyes.

When you're willing to help, you'll find there's a need. The people around you are crying out for what you have to give. This is why God has placed you among the people who surround you. He knew you would need them and they would need you.

You can be a ray of light to brighten someone else's shadows. You can be a whiff of sweet perfume, a drop of refreshing rain, a spoonful of nourishing honey. You can be the face of Jesus to someone searching for the truth.

Who knows? Maybe you'll be the one he chooses to help lead them home.

Is there any greater wonder?

Laundry Lines

By Dana Portillo

I could tell you of loss and heartache
of disease and suffering
of sirens that run
through urban neighborhoods at all hours
but instead I will tell you
that my laundry is out on the line
for the first time this year
the windows are all open
and my peony and rose bushes
(which I did not plant but merely enjoy)
are all bursting with buds
And most of all I will tell you
that despite whatever personal injury
I have knowingly or unknowingly
caused on the world,
there's a God
who calls me his beloved
and says
"yes, even today."

Relishing the Ordinary

By Lauren Carrizal

My son reaches for my hand: "Mama."

As his hand clasps mine, I'm immediately drawn into this moment with him. We walk side by side along the river, strolling slowly amongst the tall grass. He points out a duck; I nod and acknowledge his small voice in this loud world. He has such an eye to see the world for what it is, something that I'm still learning as an adult. The wind blows through our hair and the Texas sun shines down on us, warming us like an embrace. As we go, I'm pulled into the simplicity of just being with him—both with him and with Him—within these ordinary days.

These simple and small moments. These intricacies of place and experience interwoven within my present time.

Have I missed it all before this? Have I missed all that life could offer me because I was too busy, too serious, or too rigid? The draw toward simplicity pulls me tighter; I'm less able to resist its urges.

Perhaps being a mother is to have your eyes opened to the Spirit's movement within this world. It is to fall into a life of simple goodness to be reminded of the world God created just for us. It is to experience the wonder and awe of our children as they encounter this world for the very first time.

I've often been too serious, too cynical toward this weary world. But I've also been wide-eyed, open to wonder, and curious. When I was a child, I saw the world as a place to explore, my backyard another puzzle piece that fit just right that was filled with things to see and hold onto.

I sense that I've lost that childlike wonder toward this world as I've grown older. It has stifled my creativity and the pull I feel toward art and beauty. I fret over the mundane tasks of adulthood: laundry needing to be done, the floors that need to be swept, dishes that need washing, the plants that need watering.

When did I last clean the bathrooms? What do we need for groceries this week?

But I sense myself beginning to wonder again.

Where is the beauty in this? How can I make this place beautiful? Where is the goodness in this ordinary yet messy life? How is the Spirit moving in my midst?

My son turns four in a few months, and as the years have passed, I continue to watch him in awe. The way that he sees this world as worthy of exploring. The kindness he shows on a daily basis. The simple prayers he speaks and the songs he sings when he thinks no one is listening. The way he squeals over dandelions and calls them "so pretty."

Am I awake to this life and God's hand within it?

I'm coming to life with the spring buds and blooms. I'm relishing this ordinariness, this simple life. Perhaps it's been here all along.

May I have eyes to see it and a heart that beholds it with the admiration it deserves.

Flour-dusted Fingertips

By Allana Walker

Flour-dusted fingertips and dough beneath my nails: These are life's simple blessings.

At night, I stir my starter, feeding it with flour and water, and let it rise. In the morning, I am greeted by happy little bubbles, the smell of warm yeast, and a reminder that transformation often occurs in the dark hours of the night.

I mix my dough in a big glass bowl: starter, water, flour, salt. Stir. Cover. Let dough rest. And I am reminded that I, too, need rest. To sit, to breathe, to settle, covered by my Maker's grace. To let all that is stirred up within me work its way into my soul and take shape within my heart.

Four times—every hour, on the hour—I stretch my dough and fold it. Every time I uncover my bread bowl, I see the dough has risen a little higher, and I am reminded that I, too, cannot rise without discipline and care. I cannot grow or change if my soul is never stretched.

Now, I wait. For three long hours, I leave my dough to finish rising. 10,800 seconds tick by, reminding me that sometimes in life, as in baking, all I can do is wait.

What do I do in the waiting—not for the temporal bread I crave, but for the spiritual, for the eternal?

Weep.

Sing.

Laugh.

Pray.

Trusting that some good will come from this longing, that my Maker knows the recipe for sanctification, that the waiting is part of the process, and my soul will be better for it.

Seven hours from the time I mix my dough—seven, that number of completion—it is time to shape my loaf. Onto the flour-dusted countertop it plops, no longer the sticky mess it once was, but something new. Cohesive, malleable, full of life. After my waiting, I, too, will become something new. The joy and the sorrow have blended together in my soul like flour and water. I have been stretched and folded, tested and tried. Wisdom, like yeast, has worked its way through my heart and mind, transforming me.

Then comes the most painful part: *the score*. Knife in hand, I pierce my dough, and the sharp, steel edge of my blade carves a crescent moon into the heart of my loaf. It grieves me to scar my creation, but without this severance, the bread will not rise. In the heat of the oven, it would morph, misshapen. So it is with my soul. Sometimes, my Maker must pierce my heart with his gentle blade, carving furrows of compassion into me so my soul does not become misshapen.

Into the fire my loaf goes, tucked into the cast-iron cradle of my Dutch oven. As I set the timer on my stove, I am reminded that I, too, am safe amid the fire. The flames will burn me only for a short time, for my Maker knows precisely how long I need to be refined. I will emerge from this trial unscathed, wholly different.

At last my loaf emerges, and the soft smell of baked bread fills my kitchen. Now is the time of feasting and rejoicing. And so it will be in the end, on the day when my Maker's labor of love is complete. The hunger pangs of my heart will at last be satiated, and I will rest at my Maker's table.

Flour-dusted fingertips and dough beneath my nails: These are foretastes of grace.

Poetry

September Rain

By Michelle Stankos

I fell in love with September rain
Flush of pain
Release of the strain
Orange and rust lay soaked on the ground
Their beauty all around
Thick fog hugging the city like an old friend
Hiding what's beyond
Exposing what's within
I fell in love with September rain
The light tap, tap of clouds crying gently
Releasing the weight of heartache and pain
I fell in love with September rain
And I would do it all over
Again and again

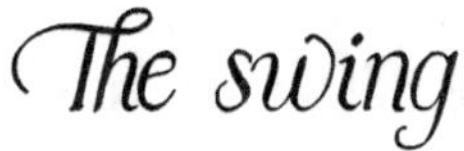 The swing

By Bernadette Lamb

Isn't it something
How the sun shines through strands of hair
Like the warm glow behind an earlobe?

Strokes of paint can't
Quite convey the feeling of
Weightlessness

When rusted chains press into palms
And the white sun blinds as
The known world slips
Away

Do you remember when your worst enemy
Was a terrorizing cloud of mosquitos and
Not
The crippling fear that
You are not enough?

Agate Hunting

By Ali Noël

I recommend it. Combing through winter
waters of the Oregon coast. Searching for
stones that point me to Jesus. You can see
it, in the lines. A love of beauty in the hidden
things. The forgotten things. Truly, if we do
not cry out, the sunlit stones of Lincoln City
will proclaim the glory and wonder of God.
The squeals of my children as the seafoam
dances along the shoreline remind me, *the
joy of the Lord is our strength*. Let me never
forget the God-given weapon of silliness. The
shield our laughter makes against the bitter
schemes of darkness. Help me to remember
how the Spirit met me here—searching for
stones, and finding Jesus.

Smallflower Desert Chicory: an Auguring

By Laura Vogt

I thought you were a daisy,
your bright splotch of almost-neon yellow
in the emerald and lime grass.
It was just you, alone. *Oh no, don't pick
that one*, I told my son, his fists full of dandelions—

some blooms bursting cotton clouds, others stiff coils
of yellow, the petals held taunt, as if they would never let go,
as if they knew that too soon they'd dissolve into solid white steam,
ephemeral, illusory, ungraspable. *See*, I cupped a spikey-lobed
leaf, *there's only one bloom. Let them grow.*

I showed him a barren stalk of chicory, noted
the similar leaves, prophesied that many more blooms
were arriving. He didn't listen. He took off,
wavering down the trail, in a fog of dandelion seeds,
in pursuit of his own inexpressible phantasy.

Smallflower desert chicory, *Pyrrhopappus
pauciflorus*, false dandelion, because one must crouch
close to spot the difference, or so the wildflower
field guide foretells—but aren't you much grander
than your cousin, much broader and brighter.

And, says the book, your stems have branches,
while dandelion only has her leaves. Your home,
wide prairies, disturbed spaces. I caught you beneath
a canopy of oaks, before that elm that toppled
the spring before last. Disturbed spaces.
We walk on home, leaving you luminous and lemon-

yellow in the brush, and there, along our woodland
path, I glimpse several more chicories—your sisters,
far-flung, a vast distance away from you. I study
their form, thin oval petals circling, a repeating medallion

of florescent chartreuse. Stems, olive-green
and bristly. Their faces lifted up towards
the overstory, caught in morning shade,
longing for afternoon sun. There is stillness,
in the forest, their bodies at rest.

Yet I feel tension—between the wayward lunges
of the groundcover and the chicory's roots:
they grasp underground, perhaps divining for minerals
or for magic, for what's hidden. There is something,
in the air, that feels like an auguring.

A tautness between what's observable and between nebulous
fantasies. We wind alongst the forest trail, on a quest for the citrine
and moss hues of small flower dessert chicories, unsure
what sorts of prophecies are unfolding this day. And I listen,
as my son prattles on, question layering upon question, all futures
just as clairvoyant as an auguring of chicories.

Perhaps, A Moment of Stasis

Along the rise, mint stalks of fourwing saltbrush
and feathered umbrellas of flaxen-brown

drooping brome tremble and bow,
whisked beneath the gasp

rushing off down from the precipice and across
the rolling meadow. The cliffside, unmoving,

seemingly unchanged—and yet,
rock and sediment rotates

to brush against the texture of sunlight, evolving
over millennia into something new. Into the moment's

inertia, against the muted rumble
of earth, the vibrating creak,

then gape of boreal chorus frogs begins again. And
the sunglow spreads wide, soaking across the expanse,

reaching along the gorge's curve
to intertwine with shadow, to press

against that borderline of dark. The terrain lapses into
hesitation—only the grasses snapping, then quavering,

then within balance. And down
along the valley, a woman

sways on the porch swing, absorbing all that is given,
withdrawn into the promise of possibility, caught between

where a memory is shaped
and refined, wondering if there's

a way to remake the future, wondering if she should
even try. The air scents of damp, of mineral and

faraway waters. And she knows, there is
no such thing as stillness, as stasis.

The Saints and Poets Say

By Megan Willome

long live ordinary time
amid ordinary tiny wildflowers
live long plain days
full of minutes
they go fast, the weedy weeks
look their wonderful in the eye
let us set this rock and that one
beside one another
see if they strike up a conversation
about the usual things

Mountain Bluebird

Two mountain bluebirds settle
in the lettuce, as if salad bar
was their natural nest.
I beckon them and one lands
in my hair, digs in its toes.
(It does not hurt.) *So, I shall
henceforth live with a bluebird
for a hat.* Thank you, bright thrush,
who dove into my brain
ate up my insects
homed into my cavity
with blue song.

Ducklings

By Sandra Rose Hughes

I want to remember three shining brown heads
Bobbing above clean, bright uniforms
As I walk them to school, pushing the baby in a stroller.

And the girls are holding hands
(such small, soft, hands,)
As they run downhill in the morning sun,
Their hair cascading, gleaming like waterfalls
Over shoulders like slender mountains,
And the boy rides his skateboard, alongside me
Falling off every few moments, and trying again,
And I wince, hoping he doesn't ruin the knees of his new school khakis.

Clean, freshly washed brown heads
All in a row with matching uniforms
Like so many little ducks.
All my hopes, my dreams, my everything,
And I walk them to school and release them into the world.

the stillness of trees in winter

By Kristen Avila

mirrored in the face of one who has gone silent
  who has lain a fortnight in solitude's candlelit parlor
    likening death, gentle and sweet as the touch of a parent, long parted
     weaving crowns from that great ivy curtain, divine peace beyond—

then, morose, returned to the task of sweeping floors, stirring pots
  with the same wooden spoon used to carve
    that gaping hole
     in the pit of a stomach

which gazing long out frosted windows cannot fill
  where not a fresh kiss on a rosy cheek can revive
    crackles of that dying fire.
     still,

through tall reeds and the dreadful alignment of stars, He forges
  my path—
    before bare soul, black stone set for this very moment

as ripples break the water's surface,
  I too fragment
    each shard, an awakening

evocations of God—
    painting barren branches with the bronze hour of day
    the heat of my given palm on my beating chest
    tending to the dead
     with equal care
      as with the living.

Afterward You Will Understand

By Lucien Levant

In soil where I rarely tread
A treasure gifted, never read,
Abandoned in an office glade.
As creeping weeds of years invade
And choke the precious budding sprouts
Its title grows in rows throughout:
My God have you forsaken me?

The question wracks a seeker's mind,
Who in desperation pores to find
A fruit in that forgotten field.
A bud, abiding, bears a yield
That answers longing hearts' entreat;
Its taste to seekers' tongues is sweet:
My God have you forsaken me?

Uprooting crowded thorns of dust
To tend the tree the Lord grew thus
In secret while He seemed be gone.
The voice of God was heard thereon:
A plan, a plant, was plainly laid
To ease the hurting heart that prayed:
My God have you forsaken me?

Through yellowed pages never known
And mustard seeds in secret sown,
The harvest reaped, the words were read.
I, to the Lord, in earnest said
My God, to you affix my heart
That we may never be apart

And in my soul your roots ingrain
That I need never ask again
My God have you forsaken me?

Our Community Bible Study

I remember the night air
leaving those Friday evening neighborhood gatherings:
the cool, fresh smell between the trees,
and the heartbeat of cricket chirps outside.
Woken by mommy or daddy to go,
and groggy, led or carried to the car
from the bright living house
out into the quiet peaceful dark,
which (in secret) had fallen like a blanket.
We wobbled over lilypad stepping stones,
wishing to stay longer with friends
in the secure spirit of community.

The spirit always stayed alongside us,
and with it, I fell asleep in the backseat
to wake up only as we pulled into the driveway,
home in a blink,
and again to be gently led or carried,
this time to bed.

Day 1

By Zane Paxton

The void is split by the God of all sound,
   A symphony loud, to allow all might.
   A quake that trembles the empty to right
Itself. Filled to fullness from sky to ground.
An Eternal chord rings out, till unbound;
   The darkness theme to become our new night,
   And all will wake to the tuning of light.
Expand the refrain—the goodness lay found.

Lean in now, for a whisper is the same;
   The hum of heaven—creation leaks.
The crevice of quiet tells us it came;
   The hiss of the wind, the babbling creeks—
Harmony groans, but still crackles aflame.
   Let all who hear know; Infinity speaks.

What Long Awaits . . .

What long awaits a night held dearly still?
  A fog, post rain, and the moon to insist?
Let lights be all dim, and sounds but a trill;
  Here, dusk is too inviting to resist.
A hint of satisfaction in the air
  From the calming winds and evening birds song,
And the smell of time that moves blind and fair
  On this night—so dear, so calm, and so long.
The day has died enough to let this be

In such motion that takes dawn to twilight.
From beyond delight in what I can see
   Comes the call, "Still". A slow, solemn, invite.
      I'll sit and watch the stars ignite slowly
      Content to help this night be not lonely.

Seeds

We are dirt-mixed.
Covered and
resting in a present darkness.

All shells that fell
to lay alone; cast
and strown, and waiting.

Waiting
on a wonderful rain—
on liquid life
to satisfy all that came and might
come again—in drops
like blood from above,
To wash us and break us.

And through it,
in the rooted, dross, surroundings,
we might become something
new.
All of us, seeds
now found within a garden.

Like Dried Leaves

By Karen Swallow Prior

These

thoughts

of mine spin

like dried leaves

caught in a gust of

wind that funnels upward

turning round and round and round

swirling slowly in a cyclone of sputtering

air

that clenches into a fist that clutches

the leaves then catches its

breath

and breathes

and leaves

the leaves

alone

to float

finally

freely

gently

down

to earth

to rest

at last

again.

Royal Doulton

By Mary McReynolds

Royal Doultons hold their age,
at seventy years around the sun
still blithe and lithe with
autumn's breeze ruffling down a
silken skirt, her form
a wondrous slender slip of
however old she was formed to be,
never changed unless she fell:
See the dainty unstepped foot
peeking from the wind blown hem,
porcelain skin smooth, wrinkle free,
no blemish, strain.
She looks the same
as when we freed her from the crate
mailed from Cambridge long ago.

My Grandpa Long sent many gifts
when living in the British Isle:
toys and candies, books and dolls,
cuckoo clocks and Toby mugs,
Irish wool and little crowns
from the queen's coronation day:
things, mere things, worn thin and done.
I loved him more than I can tell
and he was old when I was young,
born that way it seemed to me.
He passed away right through the door
where people come and go no more.
My parents, too, each followed suit,
aging life quite did them in and they

are gone and now my turn to face
the music of lost time.

Royal Doultons hold their age while
mirrors show the changing truth
from first to last until we're shelved
looking at the days now passed.

Ode to the Minivan

By Amanda Nowlin

Oh, what's in a Minivan?
Oh, what does she know?
Open her doors
What does she hold?

Well...

There's an applesauce mural dried on the glass
Library books hopefully not past
due.
Lost socks. Forgotten shoes.

Mud
  Sand
    Shells
      Rocks
        Stones
          Bones
            Snacks
              A Horseshoe crab

Just his shell; not alive
Well, at least not *this* time.

Notebooks and sketchbooks
All my best pens I've been looking
For.

Coins, coins!
Unless

I need a quarter
Several bottles half full of water

A potty seat
A change of clothes
Swimsuits, sweatshirts, because you never know

Leaves and feathers
Lots of sticks
A mysterious black substance
Not sure what it is

Pinecones and shark teeth
Empty cups of coffee

Culver's coupons
But never enough
To ever get the free stuff

A soccer ball, basketball, a balance bike
Because 10,9,7 and a little tyke

Held together with duct tape and dust
This minivan, this is us.

En Los Mimbres

By Daniel Bishop

I hear the quail call en los mimbres
from cottonwood atop fence posts
  beneath sagebrush's blue-green frailty
—skinks with blue tails dusty and skittering at their roots
   freezing in hot tub puddles
    warming in hand and sun—

crying as if through unlocked bathroom door
  an intruder has
  uncovered its naked beauty
standing tall between antiphonal song
  plume arcing overhead

and you
brush in water tapping on glass
high desert rendering in gray blue
and muted green
a temple breaking out of flat plain
high priest of your childhood

    among the evening wind
   hummingbird trill decorates the air
   in swoops to and from
    sugar water in your aunt's feeder
     or its perch on bare pine limb
   off into nothingness

it darts past us cross-legged on the turf
  and I can't help but imagine
its beak like a needle piercing my cheek

its tongue on my tongue
retreating in disappointment
      at the bitter silence.

Beneath the Sanctuary Vault of Night

From the doe's dark womb, the voice of the Lord
Spangles deerskin hides and calls forth fawns into light.
At his word, her children fall like dawn upon the leaves.
The sundering voice of God kindles forests
With broken limbs, commands the bellows of the wind,
And turns his handiwork to ash.
He sets lightning's roots beneath the earth
In sintered groves of desert sand
And dredges mountains from the sea.
He wields their peaks as spears
To break sidereal pride.
His voice instructs the flying fox,
Owl, and jackal at their work,
Makes earth a bosom for their young.
For Him, their children sing 'Glory' and dance
Beneath the sanctuary vault of night.

Sonnet of the Second Coming

The hymns are sung, and quiet falls anew.
Come close, O Lord. But soft. This emptiness
Cannot withstand your splendor, though like dew
It hangs upon my twilit heart, diaphanous.
Let not the rising sun, with serpent's strike,

Usurp the glory of your dew's relief.
The morning star, which vainly taunts—unlike
The saints we've canonized for their belief—
Will fall, unholy conflagration burst
Before your holy feet. Our risen Lord
Returning, splitting heaven, nulling curse,
Will snuff that flame beneath a spoken sword.
Knowledge of good and evil shall expire
When heaven is reborn out of the fire.

Treeborn

By A. A. Kostas

here's how I remember it:
you, dashing inside with sweat beading
by your hairline
my glasses slipping down my hooking nose
dragging me outdoors gravitationally
to the base of the eucalypt

here's how I remember it:
you, laying my hand on the bulging trunk
striped with mottled skin
turning our mutual eyes skywards to be
brushed by skittering branches
leaves oiled and ready for flame

here's how I remember it:
you, with prayers like a finger plunged into syrup
stuck and covered by the presence
my body lean before the arbory
sinking into dendroid whispers
straining to sense your god

and then:
the voice comes from the core
of the rooted timber
I, too, live to please the lord

Garden Gate

By Mary Anne Abdo

Oh, sanctuary of mine.
Where the smell of earth is embedded,
into these old ragged leather shoes.
And black gold melds into my palms—
Each line tells many garden enriched stories.
A brave gardener never needs gloves.
To reach that thin veil of our souls.
Craving to touch each intricate membrane,
of these garden gems.
Pulling weeds as if each fibrous root,
eradicated troubles from the day.
Protecting and nurturing every garden wonder,
for our eyes to behold.
Daydreaming in winter—
Ribbons of snow pile up against,
this magical entrance of tranquility.
Plans to sow each precious seed.
Patiently waiting for spring to awaken.
Always drawn to this small parcel of land.
A refuge for birds,
pollinators,
and kindred-spirits.
Sustaining us with the seeds,
of faith,
hope, and love,
each and every year.
Opening this wooden gate is the entranceway,
into a slice,
of God's paradise.

Vessel

A room full of memories.
A place of quiet contemplation filling the soul and seizing the day.
A structure that embodies every season.
A composition of windows where nature plays.
A construction enabling the poet to write, capture, and paint.
A framework that holds God's essence.
A solarium assembly of animals that are admired and loved.
A configuration of a mind in tranquility.
A manor to which my deepest thoughts,
     have awakened this mystical pilgrimage.

Scenic Overlook

By Lee Kiblinger

It is miles before we pull over—
the curling roads cart our cramped bodies
to where our world thinks we should go
and we peer through the familiar frame
of the windshield at the gray pavement
winding up the pass; we sit restless

behind glass, missing all of the signs:
the refrain of mountain river-song,
a redtail mounting the aqua sky,
the golden regattas of aspens
flapping high over sea green valleys,
all waving, *Over here! Come and see!*

For us, detours are a squandering,
of restraint, a kiss with a missed
turn, a brush with a jam of strangers,
a rock to crack our taut windows,
frighten our maps free from their folds
and take our fixed eyes from routine roads

that train our leadened hungers and hearts
to slow for the rudimentary,
the plea of some mass-formed image:
two words and a simple stick figure
peering through a tiny telescope—
Scenic Overlook, it says to us

*if only we could hear it, begging
us to roll down our tinted windows,
to blow free the hair from bleary eyes,*

invite us to waltz with rolling hills,
wave back to the pines and hum our hymns
with the steady rhythms of rivers—

but the board just offers an exit:
to park and walk toward the cemented
edge, the concrete for stiff travelers,
for those who ignore behind the glass,
the unraveling beauty they pass through
the panes of the safe and forgotten.

Grandfather's Visit

a psalm of ascent

Our Pops still missed the door to his guestroom;
he walked his chocolate pie to the garage
chanting, *this is my house, I know my way.*

We witnessed his own wits and ways unhinge
from today, as the doors swung too wide,
turning handles to the past or imagined.

He begged to invite his dad for supper
and paced along our windows, hailing
the unknown neighbors with backdoor hellos.

Hundreds of boxed memories were tossed,
flashbacks from Asian trenches were spilled
with sentence fragments and indefinites.

We wanted to plug these portals, slow-close corks
to keep thieves from what's lucid, what seduces
a broken mind through its threshold.

But age shut the door on the rational,
and words twisted into confusing knots
that we struggled to loosen and unlace

Until that third day . . . when our sabbath doors
flung open to a world unclocked and staid;
where the spirit unlocks our penned-up place

And those first notes of the well-worn hymn
were love-transposed, so our Pops' voice
rose—above the time, unlatching to find

the door of ushered words sung true—
where psalms approach the waiting gates
of then and now and what will be new.

The Eucharist as a Coloring Page

By Caroline Liberatore

We are halved before the holy
Of holies, unclasped
Palms clammy with crust
Craving color and unquenched

You tower before us in
Cobalt and crimson caricatures
A dialogue of this dinner
Pigments bleeding towards totality

Surely
One drop would color this water
                              into wine
Surely
One blot will bleed unleaded glass
                              divine

And the toddler bounces
Brazen on the kneeler at this
Bows buoyant in her braids as
She awaits the great splattering

Sunrise

You will see it if you strain
Just beyond the grayscale rooftop
Of the shopping center that was
Just repainted over the forest green
A bit too gauche for this decade they
Just decided. You will see it after
You blink away the neon gasoline sign
Just driven by, garish but nothing
Like the cathedral spreading its arms
Just up ahead. Yes, here you will see
It, housed above golden-capped domes
Just gaudy enough to embellish the sunrise.

Mirage

Are we to love that which is
not real? Then I love
trees swimming in the creek,
their slender bodies
melting into another supple
portrait, this one spackled
with honey and moss
intermingled with mud.
I think they feel
like silk, I think
they know of tenderness
that is endless.

Twilight Baptism

By Heather Cadenhead

The curve of the moon is my headcovering
as I repeat liturgies, shivering. Wet clothes
clinging to skin and scabbed knee, bone-dry
throat a testament to my persistent thirst.

Cold rivulets collect and blur creeds,
each vow bleeding into the next. Fishtail
braid damp against my back, I consider
the stone-deaf stars. Constellations

like catechisms recited
by a careless congregation—
their light my only relic.

realizing

By Emma Michael

I must have dreamed for a new pair of eyes
        between wandering redwood
forests   and imagining a recipe for lemon cake.
Upon waking

caught the dust of sleep memories rolling in the rays
from the window,
blinked them   to the tune of "Amazing Grace"
recalled a past I never noticed:

Words with lips that whispered   in color,
      swirls of hot sky on the horizon,
a bouquet of lullabies, Monet's lily pads   grinning,

the pinkish delight of an ice-cold nose,   spoons
tinkering   in the hollows of teacups,
spattered rain on the skylight,   a jar of honey
glistening,   warm lilies on the wind–

the opus of Abba   a web of living tissue
ever-creating   after its Creator.   I must have
dreamed for a new pair of eyes   and

for lips with words that whispered in color,   must
have thought eyes were only for seeing when
I wished it,   must not have
known I was   aching   when I dreamed it.

Devouring this experience, lids shocked
agape   by grace,   my drink with them,
sniff with them, hear with them eyes.

Two Lenses, Two Haikus

By Kris Ann Valdez

Like a mariner,
hope clutches a telescope,
waits for future lands.

Magnifying glass
in wonder's hands, observes all
that already exists.

Clichés

By Camilla Richardson

At eight, I became a cliché,
Gazing at the stars
From my swingset,
Wondering if my soldier brother saw them
From his army tent.

I looked at the moon and thought,
He must see its half-shape tonight,
And the big dipper's massive stretch across the dark.
Up there, where our eyes met,
We were together.

Storytelling

Walter Benjamin claimed that storytellers
Find their roots in fairytales.

There is little missing in a story,
Besides an element of magic,
That keeps it from being of the fairy sort.

What is that magic, then,
Except for a bit of wonder woven through the plot?

A Cup of Winter

By Abbi Bodager

As I stroll through this periwinkle
landscape, it's hard to believe
I'm about to leave it all behind.

The thought doesn't hurt, exactly.
It's more like falling back
into a cool bed of snow,
like the powder surrounding me.

Winter is solemn.
She isn't vibrant like her sister, Spring.
And yet, she holds a sharp beauty all her own.

So today, I want to breathe in the silver air,
and stay attuned to my senses.
For even bittersweetness is a cup
half-filled with joy.

Sudden Joy

What is this radiance
in my bones,
like flowers blossoming
out of dead flesh?

I don't deserve such delight.
But oh – how marvelous
to cup it in my hands,

to hold it to my mouth
and let the honey drip
down my throat
until I am nourished and free,

satisfied by abundant Love.

Tender

Whenever my soul is tempted to harden —
Lord, keep me tender.

Run your palms over my heart,
softing the corners
and shaping the fragile places.

I might shriek at your touch—
but, even so, please
don't let me go.

Though this metamorphosis may shake me,
I don't want to settle for a half-formed life.

I want to yearn, and cry, and love, and grow,
to respond to the world like a clapping child—
so, Lord, please keep me tender.

Abraham Had a Grumpy Wife

By Stacia Priscilla

What was Sarah thinking
when she laughed at God?
Does she think there's anything
too wondrous for the giver
to give, too good to believe?
What about the whole
-grain bread you ladies had
this morning? The faith you had
when you were just a little girl?
And when God finally brings about the bundle
in her 90-year-old womb, would she give back
to the giver for every wondrous thing
she had? As any human lady would,
Sarah wouldn't budge.
Thank God her husband did.

Pearls

By Dorothy Nielsen

I wasn't asking for advice all those years ago
when I mentioned the brick wall I'd hit.

But you know parents: they recall times
when a band-aid and a hug instantly cured most hurts.

So when I described my wrong turn,
dead end, impossible dilemma,

they needed to solve it at once, before I left.
The best first-aid for me, they believed, was their faith and wisdom.

They were right of course (or mainly right at least).
But try telling a twenty-one-year-old daughter

anything. Especially that graying parents
are custodians of plenty of useful stuff

collected over decades of battering against
then circumventing or dismantling piece by piece

their share of brick walls. Not to mention
the countless ditches they've dug their way into and out of.

At her age, the young woman only sees the distressing dust
and grit underneath their well-scored nails.

At twenty-one, after all, the world's her oyster bed
offering up smooth, ready-made jewels

to anyone young and resilient enough to plunge her face
into clear waters - which back then I thought for sure I was.

"I wasn't asking for advice,"
my twenty-two-year-old said last night.

He rolled his eyes, sighed, then clammed up.
I gave him a strained smile and awkward pat on the back

then took myself off. From the dresser top
I picked up the crystal oyster shell

sent from my sister seven years ago
in celebration of my last chemo treatment.

I whispered a cascading prayer of gratitude
as I ran my finger along its biting erose edges

and over the small iridescent pearl inside.
Then in my mind I fingered the invisible strand

my parents had bequeathed to me.
I imagined it over slow decades slipping into my hands

from their gritty fingers as it was being formed
painfully, bead by blessed bead.

West and East

Mile upon mile of preternatural silver-black
iced with ivory peaks—I gulped it in
from thirty-thousand feet above B.C.
without any obligation to share my private awe
with the stranger in the aisle seat.
It was the kind of airy solitude
I thought I'd needed for decades married to
the most sublime earthly sight
granted to me in all my fifty years on,
or occasionally high above,
this scrabbling planet.

But if forced to choose,
I'd trade this lofty memory for that ten-minute snippet
of earth-bound beige, white, and blue prettiness
early one morning a long way back
on Lake Michigan's eastern shore—bare feet
tickled by the marram grasses, sinking
ankle-deep all the way up our climb over shifting sheets
of sole-burning heat until we reached
the sweet spot from which to fling our bodies
down the other side,
turning untroubled over and over in that final free fall
before we landed together one month later
at the foot of St. Anne's altar,
somersaulting just one more time
down the almost fluid dunes to come to rest
in laughter on the soft white sands, and simply
entrusting ourselves entirely—
as we've had to, since then, countless times—
to His blessed gravity.

All I Could See

All I could see
from where I stood
was sky.

Well, sky
and a sward of grass
across which a dog was racing,

chasing something perhaps?
A stick, maybe. Or a 10-year-old boy,
or the memory of a 10-year-old boy.

But it was the sky I couldn't look away from.
Well, the sky and the blessing
of a 10-year-old boy racing through grass.

Dawn Redwood

The only conifer whose needles fall in autumn
shields me from a sudden late August rain
though a drop or two
blots my page.

All I used to be has fallen away. Most days
I can see nothing behind that's not brittle
or broken, nothing ahead not
some shade of gray.

The rain pauses. I don't move.
For now it's here, in time,
You've placed me
anyway.

Longfellow's Home

By Hannah Sanders

I can almost hear the walls whisper.
The old home sighs, settling
into itself, floor yielding obligingly
under my footsteps in gentle squish
of carpet and wood, the embrace
of one who has lived long and loved much.

A docent reads his Hymn to the Night aloud
into his empty study, where perhaps
he exhaled this song from depths of woe,
from aching hollow where love reposed.
Did he, pacing by this desk and chair,
ask to bear, say his untranquil prayer?

What cares penned here were slipped aside
for Children's Hour, bracing, beckoned
into hope by arms eager, entwined? Here
a fortress stood once, breached by tender love.
What hallowed habitants these walls have held,
these fireplaces warmed, these kitchens fed!

Upstairs, where his last words were said,
we sit cross-legged on the floor by his bed
to hear The Bells of San Blas. I see him there
perched on a rock, on a distant shore,
Little Fanny on his knee, watching ships roll
into light. It is daybreak everywhere.

Homebody

Monarch butterflies appear
sunlit gold
in our backyard, and my son
beckons;
we watch in quiet rapture
as they drink the abundance
of last week's weeds
we meant to mow.
At first just a pair,
and then we count seven
that are held to our home
on their ancient path.
So I lie amidst purple-white blooms
we didn't sow
to rightly number
the riches of our home.

Zuzu's Petals

By Sarah Elizabeth

My prayer is that we always remember to

Hold onto this dear, dear life
These minute pieces of heaven
Absent-mindedly stuffed in the corners of our hearts
To be rediscovered in a month, a year, a decade

To give our souls the courage to take
One more step, one more breath
To dream one more dream
To believe he is good, more than good

To declare that it's really true:
What a wonderful life we live.

Only a Moment

So we hold these days
Like petals between our fingers

Like everything dear to us in this world, but
Like sand: the more we clench it, the less we hold

Road Trip

Purple haze
Powdered-sugar fields
Pine trees and ones with dead leaves
Clouds cling to their sheets of shadows and groggily hit snooze
As God touches the sky and turns up the brightness,
Making their forms glow

A gray Honda and I play car tag
Turn the bend going 75
Meet a burning ball of orange
And I think of burning eyes,
Framed with white and light,
That walk golden streets reflecting himself:
Light of the world—
The sun made flesh

Summer Rain

By Dana Portillo

Do you know
that when August skies open on the Deep South
when sturdy white canvas billows
transform into gray mesh sieves
when lofty burdens are released to the earth
giving the job to the rain itself to gather,
electing forerunners and end dwellers
to hurry along to streams,
rivers, oceans

there is someone hunched under some retail awning
captured in the middle of her
hurried distraction, palms clenching grocery bags
muttering under her breath about
how inconsiderate and inconvenient the weather is
who suddenly looks up and out

suddenly she feels the primal sensation of
damp skin, smells the scent of earth
reciprocating to the skies
she remembers the smell of the juniper tree
by her walk, and the hollow sound of children's feet
running down a boardwalk
remembers the sound of her grandmother's rocker
on a pine porch and the feel of perfectly worn
linen tea towels

her hands loosen their grip
shoulders turn up and out
muscles give up their tension

inhale, exhale, repeat
a holy pause
staring past the ongoing blanket of washed out gray
a child of earth once more

Beside the Peony

I am afraid that
like Solomon's song,
you will come
in the spring and call me away

If you came in winter I would
most gladly obey, leaving
the dimensionless, wasted world

In autumn I would take no greater joy
than to walk with you
under the fiery red maple

And who in summer
doesn't long for the shade
of a garden in the cool of the day

But spring . . .
Oh, but in spring I am afraid
I'll be sleeping next to the peony
as its round orbs take shape
I'll still have a mouthful of praise
for the snowdrops who have come and gone
and a wink for the beguiling tulips
Yes, what if in spring you call me
and I linger too long at the lilac
still too simple to understand that

even greater aromas await me
once I take your hand
and live where spring is eternal

Sandhill Cranes

When I hear the sound of sandhill cranes
cutting through the atmosphere
claiming their place among aircraft
I look up and I know
exactly where they're going

Back to where the moist air is quantified,
sucked in by the mouthful
Inhale, exhale, inhale, swallow
Body gathering all the minerals the city
has slowly stripped away
while you sit under the yellow beating sun and listen
to the unified voice of moving water

These Bubbles Don't Pop

By Gloriaea

It's not gas
Are you sure?
Quite

Carbon dioxide doesn't expand my heart
Breathing in helium
Floating the organ to the roof

Not a noble enough description
For the treasured feeling
Of being held

Not a pleasant enough expression
For the gratitude welling up
To drown my eyes in light

No
It's peace beyond comprehension
It's . . . joy
Straight from my Abba

Stayed on Love

By James Robert Kibby

In the garden, kneeling, bowing, reaching.
Lord, have mercy. Lord, you know me well.
Hush my buzzing, help me hear you breathing
In the air between each ringing bell.
Eyes are prone to wander in your presence,
Play with shapes and shadows on the ground.
Help me see the light, sprung of your essence,
In my heart and in the world around.

You are always in the garden walking,
Waiting, watching, calling us to come.
We, your dear belovéd, though not tending,
Still, you sing and never cease in song.
Never will I know such peace unending;
Never, 'til my mind is stayed on love.

Half Days

Half days are snow days;
Boots dripping in the basement;
Coffee maker pouring my inner coat
While I shed this outer one.
Love enters with complaints
And a leg wet from slush,
But some space, and a warm bath,
Are Gilead's balm.

Cartwheels

By Sara Kay Mooney

My neighbor calls to tell me to stay
inside. *Lock your doors*, she says.
There's a gunman on the loose. A
chopper thrumming above confirms.

It's early afternoon on a Thursday,
and our backyard peonies just unfolded—
elegant, gaudy, blushing orbs
of lavish petals fanning in the sun.

I wonder if my son, whose school
you can see from our yard,
is on lockdown right now, shades
drawn, kids huddled and shushed.

Work is insatiable, I fear
my son's fear, and a half dozen
cop cars line our street when I leave
to get my daughter from preschool.

Despair threatens to pull
me under so I do what I know
to resist: go to the library.

Yes, it's terrible, but also the peonies,
also my neighbor who thought to call,
also the library and the books,
also my daughter—her spunky,
feisty self—turning cartwheels
at the check-out desk. And look:
the librarians—smiling, applauding
as she takes a bow.

Locking Myself out of My Office on a Frosty Morning

By Justin Lonas

Don't write a poem about this—
Not everything is significant.
Sometimes you just lock yourself out,
Sitting on the cold doorstep hoping
Someone will let you in soon.
Sometimes there is no great meaning but
A cold rump, a little shame,
And a minute to gather stray thoughts.
You aren't having a crisis
Or seeing some precious dénouement
Of the story of your life.

But sitting watching the way
Golden leaves fall from a frost-burned elm
Across your car's cracked windshield,
Or morning glazes an old city
With that fancy new place shine,
And smelling the way the cold cleans air,
Transfiguring a moment—
For a moment—to a simpler truth,
How could you not tell of it?
When the world reveals you to yourself
How could you not write it down?

On a Falling Star

My daughter came downstairs carrying a star.
Not a fiery ball of cosmic fusion,
Just a plastic sticker that glows from the wall,
One of a consolation constellation
To keep a bedroom just bright enough for sleep.

"It fell," she said, shaking it down to the floor.
"What wish are you going to make on it?"
"You can't wish on it, Dad. It's too small for that.
You can only wish on real stars—a big one,
Or a galaxy, which has billions of stars."

"What would you wish upon a galaxy?"
"Well, we live in a galaxy right now,
And our earth is the only planet with life."
"So your wish is to be here with all the trees
And bears and bees?" She smiled with toothless knowing.

Night Ocean

By Debra Fair

To praise a night ocean,

    you need whitecaps

        and bubbles on balconies

    to blow soapy spheres

from condos to shore.

    You need the waves crashing,

        smashing shells on the sand,

    pushing horseshoes to beach grass,

and lights of cargo ships,

    glimmering rainbow rays

        off colored containers

    like disco balls spinning

on the ocean floor.

    You need warm, westward wind

        to toss frizzy, humid curls

    from brown freckled faces

and lobster red shoulders.

    You need open arms to the sea,

        embracing the salty breeze,

    releasing your grasp on the rail,

to praise a night ocean.

Do You Hear the Birdsong?

By Elizabeth Wickland

Last night
we were laying in bed
when my husband
rolled over and said,
"Do you hear birds?"
I said I heard
the laundry
dragging itself along
the inside of the dryer
as it turned.

My grandparents' neighbor,
Doris, once said she heard
birds in the chimney.
Her in-home helper confessed
they weren't birds—
she'd had a baby in the night
without knowing
she was pregnant.

Poems are like that,
insisting on being born,
heard, making themselves
known
as soon as we're quiet
and still. We hear
birdsong in the ordinary,
and it sings us awake
in the dark
until the ordinary becomes
miraculous.

Dandelion

I am a dandelion,
tight fist
turned in upon myself,
and the sun calls me forth
to unfurl,
reflect back on itself
bright ray upon bright ray
opening ever wider
stretching ever higher
until I can no more.
And as I lose my luster,
faded, withered,
turning back into myself,
a stillness comes
for I have spent all I have
to give.

And still the sun shines,
turning me inside out
into an explosion of new life.

Ruach
blows, sometimes
gentle, sometimes fierce
and I am
broken
    blessed
        given
seeds in the wind.
And the kingdom grows
by no work of mine,
just the sun and the wind

who send out
and call forth.

When I am empty
of all I was given to give
and can neither turn in
or turn out
only then am I turned into
the ground
and laid to rest.

Without Ceasing

How do we pray without ceasing
if cooking is not prayer
if weeping is not prayer
if sweeping
and dishes
and laundry
are not also forms of prayer?

How do we pray without ceasing
if our work is not prayer
if our hobbies are not prayer
if typing
and skiing
and being
are not also forms of prayer?

How do we pray without ceasing
if every moment is not holy?
If every step is not on holy ground?
If every bush is not burning?

Path of Totality

By Danielle Page

shadows elongate as filtered blues and greens deepen.
awakened early, toads croak and bird song softens,
beckoning for clarity, their calls a lingering question.

so it is with the Spirit: a shifting moon aligning with
our given state, revealing shades we thought nonexistent,
suspending time and laying our very beings bare. silently
passing by, an eclipse, blinding, beautiful, gone.

The Aftermath

We are the sea foam
Bubbling and brewing
The beach stew—
Clams, seaweed, and crab
A salty brine of life for the
Scavengers of the shore

We are the precipice
Of the crescent and crash
The sand swirling in our
Retreat, we linger in the light,
Dancing across the
Shimmering sand.

We are the remnant
Of the permeable and plain
The reflection of ordinary power
Resurfacing, retracting,
Lingering, fizzling foam.

A Spider in Lavender

Out you emerged from the buds
Of my long-stemmed plant
You were much perturbed,
Plucked from your webbed home,
Evicted with every human step.

And you scuttled, in haste,
Across the desk, looking
For the garden you floated
Into that day you hatched.

I flung you to the floor,
Without the heart to
Stamp the ground where
You landed.

I imagine you will make
Your way to the roses just
A few staircases and doors away.
Your determined pace makes me
believe you are capable of
transplanting your whole self
Into new blooms; I am envious
Of the silken home you carry
within you.

Sunkissed

Lips dipped in acrylic, a glowing stain
Of yellow rim your dappled cheeks.
You remind me that our words are like apples
Of gold, shining in the sun and seeping through
Curtains of winter shade.

We wash your chubby hands and cheeks,
Shade of roasted mustard seed meant for sunsets
circles the drain, a cyclone of curiosity and infant
Innocence.

Your grin beams out and through,
Touching each mess, transforming them to
Ruby, pearl, and sapphire studded
Apples freshly fallen from the bough.

I take a bite, wipe the juice
Off my chin, and offer it to you,
Likewise.

unforbidden fruit

By Ollie Burgess

heaven is a fruit cup.
mandarin oranges without the
rind, the crusty veil—
the core would glow like the sun if set free.

and it is in a fruit cup.
all diced up for us,
in bite-sized slices so we don't choke.

the core of the universe,
bursting with light,
in munches we took as children
without realizing.

marigolds on the moon

hope is an impatient virtue.
she won't wait for marigolds to bloom
from a wasteland of mold and mildew.

she'll sit in the mud of the tomb,
and whisper to the angels who walk on the roof,
sending them to grow marigolds on the moon.

The Reality of Play

By Dabney Baldridge

When I stumble   over light-up shoes,
Take a near dive   across diecast cars,
Feel the crumbs   on my bare feet,
And see tiny socks   tossed and lost,
It's easy to feel   frustrated in the mess.
But then I remember   the reality of play
And take a closer look,   clearing the clutter
Away from my heart,   to see a child's haven,
Where puzzle pieces lay   in perfect piles
Color sorted, all,   various toys arranged
From large to small,   and cushions form
A sort of blockade.   I see stuffed animals
Put to sleep   with blankets, soft,
Stepping stone blocks   showing the way
To tea and cakes,   a lunch of cherry stew.
A rug scrunched up,   a rugged mountain range,
A banister the perfect   Grand Prix scene,
Kitchen cupboards bare,   the best hiding place,
A tower of Tupperware   taken from them.
Train tracks grow,   branching like trees,
Placemats painted   with yogurt preserves,
Windows smudged   by cheeks, all smiles,
Colored magnetic tiles   creating stained glass.
All these undertakings,   this blessed untidiness,
This Escher-chaos is   sacred childhood.

Meditation on Bread Making

Give us, this day, the bread of life broken
For us. Our human strands, he died to save;
His flesh the flour and water blood, he gave
His body to our famished souls, hands open.
Like starter fed we grow to ripe levain,
Into the dough we go, now mixed and woken.
So we are stretched and folded, coiled and cloven,
A heap to breathe and rise, then battered again.
And on the counter spilled with flour dust,
Our dough is pulled and shaped, a dome to grow
In darkness, cold. Day dawns on us with snow
And pain once more, knife scores a patterned crust
Scorched to a perfect golden hue. So we
Do rise, our holy maker now to see.

January Twilight

By Sarah Lehman

All is at peace
under a soft winter's sky
as violet melts into blue
over fields of white.

And ah, the moon!
Silently she rises
to her ancient watch
resplendent and bright.

How many winters
has she seen,
I wonder, from
her dark, velvet seat?

We are His

By Casey Sorensen

We are strong
Us mothers
Knitted in the secret place
His plans for us are good
Full of hope for our future
Our future is our children
And their children
And their children
Also, knitted in the secret place
Created in his image

We are weary
Us mothers
Because the world isn't ours
The enemy works to distract
To steal
To destroy
But when we cast our burdens
Our cares
Our life to Jesus
He holds us
Like we hold our very own

We are busy
Us mothers
From diapers
To solid food
From first steps
To first run
From drop-off
To pick-up

From graduations
To weddings
From first sight
To last
We don't stop

We are tired
Us mothers
Late nights
Early mornings
Whether
Working
Or staying home
We don't punch out
We show up
Again
And
Again
Because our love is abundant
He is our example

We are his
Us mothers
Perfectly imperfect
Loved not for what we do
But for being his alone
Strong as mothers
Weary as mothers
Busy as mothers
Tired as mothers
He sees us
He knows our hearts
Even when we feel alone
Unseen
Unloved
He doesn't forsake us
He will never forsake us

We are mothers
And we are children
His children
Knitted in the secret place
Furthering his kingdom
One child
And
One day at a time.

At Year's End

By Sara Luchuk

On a path forgotten,
     I walk
          to relive fleeting moments
              with father, sons.

The spirits of trees
     long felled
          haunt my memory and
              call to me.

They join in harmony
     with echoes
          of laughter, voices, birdsong,
              crunching leaves.

There—heron still stands,
     a remnant
          of the forest that was,
              silent sentinel.

Leaving the path now,
     I fix
          my eyes on the unseen
              and give thanks.

Joy

clear
mountain stream
gurgles and laughs its way
over rocks and under fallen logs.
rounding a bend, it leaps and
splashes its way between
slender rhododendrons.
their twisting branches reach
across the water to intertwine
and form a lacy tunnel.
filtered sunlight glances off
their broad, dark leaves and
the stream's fluid contours,
leaving behind echoes of silver.
one human watches the dance
and listens to the song
while resting in
the Maker's
arms.

Morning Glories

trash heap
filled with useless,
reeking, broken things:
looks like the inside
of my heart.

trash heap
covered each morning
with a new carpet of morning glories:
looks like God's grace,
clothing the unlovely
with glory and
splendor.

Homily

By Mary Madeline Schumpert

You skip through my dreams
echo in my sleep
sing to me in birdsong
whisper on drives home
hum in the wind
counsel through the words of a friend
tiptoe in my thoughts with the grace of song.
So much more than a cathartic monologue,
when I'm on my knees.
Answer lingering questions in the darkest days,
call out to me with crystal clarity on a thin, gold-lined page.

Always, always calling.
Always, always answering.
Always, always with me
until You come again.

So silly, so foolish of me
to call You silent.

Earth Child

By Deborah Rutherford

I.

Sleepy eyes intoxicated by desire
laced in webs, sticky and cumbersome.

Awaken earth child.

When messengers, holy and heavenly
appear in daylight, not just dreams and visions:

>	a toothless woman held a cup for money by the front door
>	of the post office
>	(her eyes were full of something I wanted.) *"God loves you,"*
>	she said,
>	and with a huff and grimace smile, I escaped to my car.

II.

On a drive down the 5, when worlds collided (literary)
as a car swerved toward mine, and there was nowhere to go;
	I closed my eyes and braced for impact—

Did I pray?

it seemed centuries (but in my mind, two lovely Angels
flew alongside my car, lifting me to safety). I opened my eyes to
wonder and relief

>	(this was the time I thought I would die alone
>	among the wreckage and burning flame...)

heart softening, eyes opening, ears listening
God woos, he calls.

III.

Things happen on beautiful mornings, like the day Mom died
as the horizon opened up on the 405 freeway when out of the blue
sky, two white doves flew toward my windshield and up to yonder,

"There she goes," I thought. And I know she's in heaven
 because God sent me two white doves to tell me so.

Star Dusk

The day yawns
as night blinks
under the star duvet:
beauty held
by the Lord's gaze.

My eyes twinkle
in His ethereal ink.

This is where I belong.
So miniscule yet infinite.
Ablazed luminaries
under the star dusk;
His heaven dust sprinkles
across the heavens
all the way down to me.

Hummingbird

By Chanda Singleton Griesë

Leafy green hibiscus bush
with flashes of delight,
whose petals uncurl red
to call out far and wide those dear
nectar drinkers come aside

I grip the steering wheel
steady in the driveway—
our white Telluride
purrs and waits for me
toes tapping the brake

my eyes returning
to spy the glass
the forward zip
and backward zag—
the ins & outs of crimson bloom

neither wasps nor bees
but a bird so small—
the size of a dragonfly
humming, strumming little bird
early morning glory sipper

calling me back to Eden's way
the beholding resting place
zip, zipping away—
keeping my mind
from the worries of the day

Doxology of Life

Why all the wonders in the world?
In the sky, the land, the oceans swirl?
Creatures diverse and separate teeming,
Migration sets the cycle streaming.

Gathering, reaching,
Through water breaching.
Carrying messages
All nature's preaching.

For breath of air and breath of life,
Prevail the whales and butterflies.
More than I can comprehend
Makes a visual Amen.

Found Poem

By Olivia Oster

I found this poem at a green lake
In the valley down the mountain
After seeing a Sunday sun rise
By a stone fire tower.
I found it in the light shining
Through the pines on the water
Waving gently in the cold breeze.
I found it on the slippery stone stairs
Down to the sluice,
Shushing in a loop of peace.
I found it in the clouds
Reflected on the still deep,
Each sky as clear as the other.
I found it in the quiet, in a hymn,
In humming along.
I found it in the verse
About radiant faces.
I found this poem in a hot sip
Of strong tea.

A Night Walk

Moth-like the moon spins her winter cocoon,
Branch-held in the black and barren sky.
Light falls, enthralls like pollen from a bloom,
Opening petals for worship on high.
Moon-struck I wander, forgetting the way,
Intangible branch words written above.
Straining in the waning dusk-light, I stray:
Worship will prove my pensive, potent love.
Forget burdens in safe cocoon-like night.
Breathe deep beyond branches, moon, mist, and stars.
Stop straining, complaining, feigning to fight.
Worship wholly; be fully where you are.
Into the empty cistern God will pour
Riches of the heavens forevermore.

The Figure of the Farm

By Mariellen Van Nieuwenhuyzen

At night when I cannot fall asleep,
I walk along the pathways of my youth.
Pulled up from deep memory,
The trails, the trees, the stones come to life.

I know that old farm as I know my own body.
The slight bend in the creek,
The stooping walnut whose arm stretches as a bridge across bramble.
Each is a freckle on the roadmap of my skin.
New folds rising and falling with weather and age,
And yet each glistens beautifully in the early morning dew.

She is not the body of my youth.
But she comes from the same blood,
And her backbone is strong.
Not even the perils of time can hide her beauty from my eyes.

No Beauty

By Charissa Sylvia

"*I see no beauty in the world,*"
someone told me recently, carelessly,
angrily demanding empathy.

I started to affirm him—a lifelong bad habit
when people speak vehemently, then I caught my breath
back to my chest, scarred already from one who has taken delight
 in weaponizing sacred things in my life,
"*everyone who speaks with passion isn't speaking truth,*" I whispered
shaking heart in my hands, stalwart hope in my mouth.

"*I love you,*" I said, "*but just last week*
I saw a rosebud born again. I saw light scatter the gray,
and the rain move across the valley, baptizing weeds and flowers alike
in the name of God, speaking of God—
I just saw him handing out sandwiches off Route 225, and you, I see you,
angry that's true, but listening still, maybe just maybe
wanting me to disagree, maybe just maybe
finding a rustle of hope rushing in on the cooling wind
and coffee-stained breath of one who still believes."

And I do believe.

With every fiber of my redeemed being,
I'll argue for beauty still, will fight
to be a thin place where it's visible.

By God, I will.

Delight Lies Just North of Your Courage

Come stretch to your breaking height,
grasp awe from among the stars,
wondrous matter factories
matter-of-factly swirling
carbon and oxygen,
calcium and iron into the world,
into *you*, you beautiful work of God
stitched together of adoration and (star) dust.

Clasp your birthright of delight
between your trembling, valiant hands—
do you feel it racing through you,
rocketing down your spine
like fingers tracing beaded prayers?

You are strong as tears now.

Ready to water the earth with your hope,
alive and eternal and irrepressible,
the spitting image of your father.

Awakened

By Pat Severin

As sunlight peeks,
I am suddenly
stirred awake
by the vibrant sounds
of children's voices.
Squeals of joy,
almost rapturous sounds
of summer abandon,
a happiness so often lost
moving into what we so
desperately yearned for.
How anxious we were
to grow up, so anxious
we counted
every year in halves,
skipping ever closer
to that next official year.
Five and a half,
eight and a half,
twelve and a half,
and then, before we knew it,
we weren't children anymore
but teens and then
adults.
How quickly we learned
that this wasn't what we
thought it would be,
rather, a place
of questions,
responsibilities

and, all too often,
WORRY.
Now in that place,
the place we had longed for,
yearned for,
we wish we could
go backwards,
wish to relive
those days of play
and childhood memories.
Had we blinked and
this is where we are?
Those voices, Lord,
happy contented voices
are your best alarm clock,
a true awakening.
I understand
why you bid them
come to you,
why their faith
was the kind of faith
we should strive for,
a faith without hesitation,
without question,
a faith of total acceptance.
Lord, as I now sit up,
wiping away
sleep's remnants,
I hear them even more clearly,
reminding me of how
my heart for you should be.
Lord, grant it for Jesus sake.

This Is How We Say Goodbye

By Liza Moore

After dark
I watched
a moonflower open,
its whole body, soft,
crept in whiteness
toward the night sky,
free and floating,
and remembered you,
last year,
falling into the stars,
your body
broken,
how it left you
dancing in the garden
listening to the moonflower
ascending,
praying
to be home
and one with the moon.

Early Morning

Heat rises
from the desert
passing through

canyon walls
the very thread
of life

which wakes
in the cholla
pronghorn

and bison
still roaming free
and like Silver Havard Agave

every twenty years
or so
I return

burning yellow
in the desert
letting this world

come back
to me as before
a flame in the soul

Hope

By Holli Gibbs

The daylight slipped away
and stripped the flame from my last candle,
but one by one the stars began to bloom
in gloomy fields of sky,
and I, though planted in the dark,
felt the spark—that old and trusty hook—
when I looked up.

Envying the Birds

Trouble swells, and we envy the birds—
the way they climb the winds with wings
and wander far and settle where
they please while we have only feet
and gravity to hold us to
the earth.
We squirm, as if our royal birth
were some mistake; we sniff, as do
the monsters at forbidden meat;
we fret and spurn our golden air;
we sigh, as if we could not sing,
as if we had no home within Your words.

Ode to Traffic

By Courtney Moody

The highway is colored
with more red flashes
than a Christmas tree.

An F-150 fills
 my air conditioner vents
with diesel perfume.

Before I can sigh like
the engine or scream
like the honks and beeps,

I stop on a bridge
and see it doubled;
arches in the sky,

seven palette stripes
painted over the waves
for angels to cross.

I see their footprints:
yellow, green, indigo,
and everything is still.

I smile in the face
of 2-hour delays,
soaking in glory

on the fastest route.

Entertaining Angels

This mortal has entertained angels (not with a glass of lemonade or a wrinkled dollar in a hat). When I walked into a street sculpture of a tin treble cleft and clanged in C-minor. When I lost my cell phone and raided every drawer as it buzzed on the dining table. When I sang the wrong stanza of "Amazing Grace" and every congregant turned to me with eyes wide as the stained glass windows while God's workers laughed all the way back to Heaven.

Perspectivally

The caterpillar spins a chrysalis, oblivious to its "why."
Skilled as Rumpelstiltskin, cautious as a child's first step.
It works. It rests. It emerges, renamed: *Papilionoidea.*
I watch its inaugural flight and describe it as a miracle.
If butterflies could speak, they would just call it: *life*.

Crafting Bouquets of Ordinary Things

*By Taylor Blayse: appears in her poetry
collection,* The Garden Daughter

When I feel too small or
plain or
afraid I should be doing
grander things,

I feel the Lord cup my cheek and shift my gaze.

My eyes wander, then, to ordinary things.

Like tiny droplets of rain
  Cascading
    along flower petals
after hot summer days.

Or small living rooms
  bursting
    at the seams with laughter and
light and
warmth,
as the feeling of home blooms in our hearts.

Or the stillness of trees.
The way they don't chase praise but
  remain rooted
    in the One
Who is greater.

So I take these moments—
I pluck them like flowers.
I arrange them and
marvel at their beauty when placed together in this way.

The Lord looks at me then, as if to say:
"I hope you craft bouquets
of *wonderful,*
          ordinary things."

The Woman is a Conductor

By Bethany Colas

She stands with her back
to a hundred faces, a pillar on a podium,
raising her baton, lifting every violin and oboe
to hover at the chin or lips of each musician, and with
the subtle movement of her wrist, conjures sound
from breath and wood that resonates,
reverberates, through the air
and through our skin.

Feet fixed, she leans into
the work, swaying, laboring, gathering
melodies and harmonies, tears and dissonance,
the apathy of lovers, a parent's fears, the weariness
of aging and the aged, bearing in her being
the wonder that the heat of summer
nights can hold all this.

She moves—the music moving
through her—then lifts her hands to hang
a single note upon the air, so clear it holds our breath
collectively, collecting all our beating hearts,
drawing silence from our burning chests
as our longing deepens
with the dark.

Mourning Light

By A.M. Everett

Mourning breaks
Through silence and stillness;
The undeniable shrillness
Of all that cannot be.

Mourning takes
What you thought your life might hold;
Stories that will go untold
And all you will not see.

Mourning wakes
To pain like the tossing
Of waves never crossing,
And never to fall asleep.

Then the Son.
Glorious freedom dispenses.
New creation commences.
Perfection at last fills your senses,
Shattering earthly offenses;
Never again shall you weep.

And mourning breaks.

4°

By Mark Rico

today's exhibit
an arctic
glaze flowing under

the laundry room door
ice forming
on shoe soles, each step

something like walking
carelessly
by the fry station

in an old truck stop
fast food joint
the scene bedazzles

drops crystallizing
to keep warm
we work fast, fingers

numbing on handles
a push broom
and a rimy mop

freezing to the floor
then ripping
away like old cloth

blindfolds torn from eyes
that grow old
to common glories

Eternity is Moments Unending

Above the humming tumult
of the ancient dishwasher
and rowdy kitchen crew—

above the murmurs
of jocund porch-sitters
and paddles splash-whacking
plastic kayak hulls—

above clicking knitting needles
and hollow smack-thumps
on the volleyball court—

above susurrating marram grass
and distant sailors chasing
the ghosts of their grandfathers
across the many-blued bay—

above children chattering by
and swimmers battling
some imagined enemy—

above our campsite
where a nest of merlins
squabbles for supper
within its cedared roof—

stratus smoke signals rise
from the southwest horizon.

Higher Than Our Ways

By Lea Emmett

Who can perceive
the atoms on the
head of needle?
Who can comprehend
the intricacies of each
snowlake fall?
Or who can know every
thought conceived by
the children of man?

We are like donkeys
in the field,
forcefully humbled because,
for a moment,
we actually believed the world
revolved around us.
A cosmic joke.

Like teaching a blind man
the beauty of the sunset,
our grasp of God's mind
is far beyond the horizon.

We yearn for the day
we will fully know you.
Unveiled and glorified,
falling prostrate
on the same ground
your hands used to
mold our forms.

In that moment,
we won't seek knowledge
or understanding of the past.
Who can want when
they have it all?

Ripples

My prayers for my
children may be my
greatest legacy.
Each a gift that
opens like the
petals of a blossom
caressed by the sun.
Will these spiritual ripples
create waves in the lives
of my great-grandchildren?
Will generations
walk in fear of God?
In freedom and hope?
Let me be
that mustard seed, Lord.
I may not see the dividends
on this side of eternity,
but I want to reap
the very present rewards
of drawing near to you.

Waking

By Lisa M. Johnson

Laid back deep,
marked beloved.
Naked self is
waking baptized–
rescued from sleep;
        bleary eyed
           human
              exposed.
Delivered
into a new day,
unable to yet speak
or perform anything
miraculous—
infant prisoner,
bound exclusively
by desire.
Eyes blink, cording tikvah
into the day's first light,
looking for the One
looking for you.
Rapacious to remain
in the soft tissue belly
of warm sheets,
belovedness
seeps—
dribbling down
onto the cold floor.

Thoughts like
pareidolia appear—

word clouds
float above:
you see *overweight*
        too fragile
            too late.
Gently soft hands
support your head,
your back—
with a resurrection
thunderclap.
Drenched now
beside Eden's rivers,
you remember—
        Before searching for God,
           God is searching for me.
I, the Vinedresser
see you
under the garden's
fig tree.
You are known
from the cradle—
utterly, completely loved
for doing absolutely—
nothing.
Your name, Beloved,
before you stand feet
to the floor—
feeling this mystery inside
your good body,
you stand.
Rising to the bedroom mirror—
      jet black hair
         silken
           dripping wet
looking into
those swollen, dark eyes.
Fully awake, you speak

inaugural words—
the morning liturgy
that is making you
a deep canyon
and say it again,
       Good morning, this is my Beloved.

A Desert Blessing

By Hannah May Schramm

My heart is heavy, burdened with leaving.
Leaving uniquely-shaped cacti and majestic red rocks.
Leaving the desert landscape in all its stark beauty.
Leaving Piestewa Peak, bathed in golden hour light.
My being drinks up the Arizona wilderness.
Such a bittersweet goodbye.

Outside my airplane window,
The Peak stands alone,
Silhouetted by the painted sky.
My gaze is fixated on brilliant hues,
As oranges and yellows intertwine.
I am captivated by the beauty.
My heart swells with joy.
Each moment brings a new collage,
I'm holding on tight to every one.

The Gray Havens' music plays in my ear,
Lulling my spirit with its wistful melodies.
I will bask in this bliss as the sun disappears,
As I fly into the cloak of white clouds.

I long to be still and rest in that splendor,
Back in the Midwest,
Back in my regular life.
Take me back and show me again.
I want a glimpse of its glory,
Oh, satisfy my soul.

But I am content in the simple blessings,
In an Indiana sunset,

In the glittering snow,
In the comfort of song,
And a blossoming spring.
I've been surprised by joy,
That blessing in the desert.
God regarded me,
And I'll never forget it.

When God Takes Your Lemons

By Caitlin Callahan

When God takes
the lemons and the bag of sugar
you were going to use for lemonade,
you then realize that the
tangerines sitting
in the porcelain bowl
at the edge of the
kitchen counter
don't make your lips pucker
or body twitch,
but taste sweeter and juicier
than the yellow thing,
and can provide
a fresh jug of
orange juice

Water's Wonder

By Leilani Mueller

She went for water, that life sustaining
Necessity. Perhaps she pulled a veil
Across her tired face. But, soul flaming
With posture straight she covers that she fails
At custom and law. Yet, she has a debt,
That still parches her throat—nothing avails.

A man sits at the well as the sun sets.
His shadow causes pause, but she abides.
"A drink, please," is his request. Confused, she
Looks at him. "Ask me for water living,"
He says. Eyes light and wait for her to see
The narrow path he walks in giving
Her the veil rending word that could command
Worlds into rhythm—redemption planned

The Cathedral

Silence becomes a whisper when you step
Across the worn-in floors and through the nave.
Click, click, click and pause—steps follow the steps
Of Saints—Those rocks who kneeling prayers gave.
Stones, each, as vast rock holding up the sky
Enwalls the centuries around this space.
You stand, small within the transept and sigh
And wonder if their lives you can retrace.

A stone, a word, you—insignificant
Among the saints that preceded your soul.

Yet, words make lines, which make significant
Each within the poetry of the whole.

Light comes down from high within this place
It lifts words into heavenly embrace.

To My Older Self

By Brianna Marshall

Don't ever forget.

The feeling of pure excitement for a warm, summer rain.
The pitter-patter of white noise on the roof as it begins.
How quickly your socks and shoes come off
And how quickly you run out to feel the warm tears of life from
    the sky.

Don't ever forget.

The joy and warmth streaming down your face as you dance.
Whenever you see the clouds roll in,
Don't feel timid, instead feel the anticipation and eagerness
For the jumping and prancing that is to come.

Don't ever forget.

Your lake at the end of the concrete driveway
And the muddy corner of the lawn.
The waterlogged dirt attempting to be a puddle in the side yard
And the waterfalls streaming from the grey shingled roof.

Don't ever forget.

Splashing in the ever growing puddles with her
And dancing the Cotton-Eyed Joe like no one is watching.
The joy that she brings you as you're filled with carefree abandon.
Being thirteen and eighteen, playing in the rain.

Don't ever forget your sister. Don't ever forget the rain.

Barefoot

By Jen Niemann

Just let me run barefoot
To watch the tulip show;
Spring fresh and dewy,
Lime leaves unfurling slow.

Let me meander barefoot
Across white crystal sands;
Ocean waves pounding,
Retreat at your command.

And let me sprint barefoot
Across a new-mown lawn,
Staining feet mossy—
Surprising glimpse of fawn!

Let me stroll on barefoot
Kicking scratchy leaves;
Crispy color crunch
Brings joyful release.

So as I trot on barefoot
Through every season of life,
Let me find your presence
The balm in every strife.

Then let me approach barefoot
Those awesome pearly gates,
Anticipating holiness,
Ecstatic in my fate.

And let me tiptoe barefoot
To bow at holy feet,
Worship and adore you
Enthroned on mercy's seat!

Then let me remain barefoot
An eternity to stay . . .
Dancing gold brick highways,
And learning humble ways.

Evergreen (What Need Have I?)

By Amber Leigh Lipscomb

What need have I for hollow things, When evergreen the Father sings?

In His refuge, my roots take root, And in His shade, my soul will sleep.

The sky may weep, yet I remain, In His embrace, I'm not weak.

I seek no more what others seek, For in His hand, I find my peace.

No need for more, no need to stray, In evergreen, I'll always stay.

Kinsman & Keeper

She gathered barley; he gathered dust, A widow's hands, an outstretched cup.

Job cries beneath the heaven's crush, A weeping man who'd lost too much.

Ruth whispers in the harvest's hush, Through fields of loss, her heart beats on.

Kinsman, Keeper, both remain, In love's redemptive, a quiet strain.

A moment still, though time may bend, In shadows deep, he holds the dawn, In silent grace, sorrow and promise entwine.

Cottage or Castle

By Christel Jeffs

*I would sooner live in a cottage and wonder at everything than live in
a castle and wonder at nothing.* —Joan Winmill Brown.

There is something in the water ripples
that churn to fury on a blazing stove,
ready for the penne or pappardelle.

Something in the warm resistance
of tearing a crisp loaf apart.

Something in the bubbling surge of
grape juice in my mouth,

the animated chorus of friends,
huddled in a home that is
peeling at the edges.

***

Something different from the
vast halls of a heart closed off

where there are self-serving platters,
low-tide vessels and
cosmetic dishes with brief curls of heat,
past their wonder.

To Make a Holy Echo

By Kimberly Phinney: appears in her collection,
Exalted Ground

What *is*
has already been done
      and *will* be done
         and will be done, *again.*

See this:

I went out walking in the woods—
beneath the Blue Ridge line
painted across the sky
and where the pink twilight
birthed just above its peaks.

There,
I found,
tangled on a beech tree limb,
a mass of golden leaves,
all airy, all see-through,
save their veiny spines—
      like the finest bobbin lace
      an artisan could weave—
to say God made it first,
      so, then, the artist could.

And there,
I found,
in the loamy, layered earth
the perfect vermillion
of a turning leaf,
bedded down in the undergrowth—

      like the red of the finest palette
        of watercolors a painter might ever own—
to say God made it first,
      so, then, the artist could.

And at last,
I laid down
in that bed of leaves,
back soft in surrender,
eyes squinted North
toward the bright, winter sun,
numbering the bare branches
that hung before me—
all fingertips and arms and hands—
reaching toward the blue belly of Heaven
just as they were made to do—
      like the dancer's body groans and moves
      or like the poet's pen sings in praise—
all to say God made it this way,
so, then, the artist could know how to pray.

Yes, we are echoing
all that *has* been done
    and *will* be done
        and will be done, *again.*

We are His holy echoes—
His *Imago Dei*—
Do you hear creation singing?
Do you hear it cry, "*Create!*"?

Heartbeat of Grandeur

By Kristine Amundrud

Black capped chickadee flits free
For a seed visits me—flap-bounding,
cavorting into cupped hands of elation

Two-note call begs that I ponder
the plain, meditate on mundane
while delight dances midair

He's got the entire world in his hands

For one glorious speck of time,
I too, feel the heartbeat of
creation's grandeur

Epistle from Heaven—in memory

Drove west past the airport, past
fallow fields clinging to a memory
Felt sorrow mount up in vivid array of color
You're no longer here

Saw a love letter written in the clouds.
Saw faint celestial words penned across
unsettling sky

If only I could make out the note, penned from forever firmament

Wind currents whip and unfurl love's declaration
Truly, clouds are heaven's kindness—
an epistle from the saints

Death never had the final word

Kenosis

God painted seashells, every intricate detail
Hung them in the Pacific for me
Radiantly streaked with chestnut brown,
fiery opals reflecting red and emerald green.

I study whorl, spires, and aperture
Pearly center of a lowly wheel shell
Mollusk, emptied of life, yet brimming over
Ocean's kenosis story to tell

God painted seashells, etched serpentine details
Washed them onto the shoreline for me
Creator's hand in everything
Brush strokes, waves, yes—even the wind in my hair
It all moves accordingly
With each exhale, I empty myself more to his will

Jeremiah 33:3

By Rachel Lynne Sakashita

This is true:
stars are songs.

The larger ones are cellos,
ocean-deeps, thunder, the last key
of a piano, a sigh of relief,
a guttural cry.

The smaller ones are silver,
lace, flutes, singular
soprano melodies, smoke
tendrils with the strength of a storm.

The diaphanous skies are a quivering
dance, a melody thrumming
with seraphic light, notes strung
onto a beam the Heavens read,

and you, who are spending yourself
in search of something mellifluous,
could spend an evening,
a whole life, and never find
this music on your own,

but hidden things are invitations.
You know this, deep
in the eaves of your spirit.
You know that you could unravel
yourself to be enveloped
by something far greater.

Reawakening

written during my eating disorder recovery

This tender body I inhabit breathes
God's breaths, lungs opening
their eager petals to an air
created just for their needs.
Is my body, crocheted and cracking
at the edges, important?
Do these earnest fingertips
of mine bear celestial weight?

They must, for through them I trace
the nebulae of God laced
into everything. This heartbeat sings
like a cathedral— the kind for sacred
things, of which I am somehow declared
both the greatest and the least.

May Sonnet

By Chelsea Fraser

The waxing spring wears thunder and the bees
Abuzz on clover heads or daffodils
That wave their yellow faces towards the trees
Drip-dropping pollen down in yellow rills.
Maybe the spring decides to stay awhile
In breezes chill and nesting birds' next clutch,
Admiring earth's bright smell and her sweet smile
Despite grey showers' oft-repeated rush.
Maybe the summer rides the wings of May
Unfolded by the thunder's roll through spring
That woke the sleeping bulb and coaxed again
The earth to stretch its branches full of leaves.
     Maybe our wonder holds the heat at bay—
     Or else Persephone, for this be May.

Revolutions

A globe forged in fire and tinged in ice,
full of balancing edges—
glacial crevasse and volcanic magma,
frozen Himalayas and impossible ocean trenches,
a core of spinning molten rock
and winds of dizzying heights—

in between, the moss and ferns abound
where water lives and neither ice nor steam;
here I can balance trees and rocks
holding in their obsidian branchings beneath our feet
a Whole whose parts are no equivalent
for the grandeur and the gall of such a place.

I burn or freeze or freeze until it burns
from summer to winter and back,
longing for the cool of autumn and the warmth of spring
to linger longer than they can,
for on this globe of fire and ice
we live not in between, but back and forth
in ever-arching lines that branch their own
obsidian words over time.

The Here and Not Yet of this whirling ball
in its pull and pushing tension
plunges people into extremes of courage
alongside limitations:
their fire and their ice,
and urge a moderation something akin to love—
to spin a faithful balance round a Sun

that burns its fire that we may live
unafraid of freezing

and burns so far that we may live
unafraid of burning—
a Sun that burns that we may live
unafraid
on a globe forged in fire and tinged with ice.

Bare

By Megan Huwa

After Andrew Wyeth's "Christina's World" (1948)

Had I known that to write my foreground, I
   must leave the farmland—I would have weighed
my whispers to the heights, my verse sung nigh,
   while tempest wrestled the barbed wire stayed.

Dressed for church but let out to pasture—
   a wounded animal left to hope alone
against the marred sun while the sky smoldered—
   I knuckled, straining my cerebrum home:

      Where the orange poppies cleave the split skin,
      the grape hyacinths jockey the sapped grass,
         the oxblood tulips upheave their silk chin,
         the blazing heads of wheat pierce forth. *Alas,*

let the glory of the dying lie bare,
   shadowing the shadow, rooted to the ground.

To The Unlikeliest

To the bubbles—
   You are beauty on an eight-lane road: glossy, round sheens of
pink and blue tumbling across gray lanes, hope-fully upward,
dodging passers-through.

To the blackbirds—
   You are marvel on an overpass: teeming hundreds, swift and
shifting as a wave, entrancing me into your tempest,
into your enclave.

To the butterflies—
   You are wonder above alfalfa fields: curtsying your pair,
a ballet in air, all clothed in white, fluttering above
the grass tipped with purple fare.

To the white heron—
   You are splendor perched in the crosswalk: Shiver away your
translucent marble yoke, stretch your neck, unbend your
smoke-blue legs, and carry forth without your cloak.

For whom were you boasting
   in the unlikeliest of places
creation's cadence and unlikely graces?

Liturgy for a Loss of Wonder

By Christina Snyder

O, my God of Wonders,
when you speak
worlds form, blind men see, and roaring winds quiet;
when you raise your mighty hand
waters part, the earth shakes, and evil perishes;
when you whisper
flowers bloom, hearts are stilled, and your spirit moves.

I know the awesome power of your Being,
yet, I'm lost in indifference and weariness
of this exhaustible, vapid life.
My sin entangles every step.
My limitations weigh me down.
My own mind hinders true sight.
Every way I turn, a distraction's claws grip me.

Father of Miracles,
I ask that you free me from
the lust of the eyes,
the lust of the flesh,
and the pride of life.

Open my eyes. Help me see once again
the splendor here on earth that
radiates from you—
the sweetness of honey,
the subtleness of growth in a blade of grass,
the richness and beauty with every setting and rising sun,
the power of the crashing waves,
the vastness of the galaxies,

the stillness in a valley of snow-capped mountains,
the gentleness of a mother with her newborn child.

May I pause,
notice,
ponder,
receive,
every good gift from you.

I ask this through the very breath you grant me each moment.
Amen.

Living

I taste the quiet snow drifting down
  and the sorrow of my empty belly
I see sweet strawberry juice on rosy cheeks
  and gray monotony on a flat horizon
I feel the thrill as my toddlers splash through puddles
  and the disillusionment of happiness as I lay awake at night
I reach out and touch the steadiness of my husband's hands
  and the cold waters of loneliness
I hear the rich symphony of boldness in the clouds
  and the snaps of desperation for control
I breathe in the scent of eternal innocence
  and I breathe out the violations of living

Changes of Perspective

By Justin Farley

"...to arrive where we started
And know the place for the first time."

—T. S. Eliot

I once looked at the ordinary
through the eyes of a restless adventurer
forced to spend eternity chained
to time and place with no room
for opportunity or change.

But time and pain and life circumstance
have a way of shrinking our field of vision
until the irrelevant is magnified
to extraordinary measures,
and new layers of life reveal themselves
beneath forms of familiarity.

Grace touches disordered hearts
with blessings of suffering
that tunnel through the rot of spoiled living
until we find ourselves back at the beginning.
There, we discover magic in the mundane;
the holy in vast, empty spaces;
beauty in stones without luster.

For we have all we need
wherever there is Light.
The greatest joys in life
are not in hoards of treasure
or mythic moments of adventure

but when the bloated corpse of self
is stripped of everything
in order to cherish the essential.

Nature's Temple

In a world where nothing is holy,
everything is profane
except the names
of secular idols
we've erected in our online temples.

Have you not been down to the valley?
Have you never attended Mass beside the creek?
Never had angels flying in the wind
plant kisses upon your cheek?
Or pressed your ear to the trunk
of an old oak to hear him speak?

Glowing screens of artificial light
pale in comparison to the natural beauty
of stars in the night—
gazing, logged off, in tune
with the key of ultimate reality.

For no one can play in nature's garden
long before their hearts become aware
of a presence dwelling there,
deeper than the earth we walk upon
and older than time itself.

In that moment, we realize
we live in a world where everything is holy
and only the material pleasures
built on the bodies of wild things profane.

For written upon every blade of grass,
every star, and every galaxy is his name.
So in this temple without doors or a roof
let us proclaim, "Holy, holy, holy."

Daily Grace

Echoes of light glow,
Resound on dawn's horizon—
Darkness heeds its call.

Yesterday is ash—
Failure burnt in the fire
Of the rising sun.

Morning has arrived.
Songbirds rouse life from its sleep—
A blank slate of grace.

I Walked with Wonder Today

By Donna Bucher

I walked with wonder today,
her pace much slower than mine.
Patiently,
she calmly showed me the way
to places I've been and
those I've yet to see.

I walked with wonder today,
her words with kindness did shine.
Quietly,
she shyly showed me his way
to places where my eyes
opened wide to see.

I walked with wonder today,
her serenity my sigh.
Silently,
she led me further away
to places of rest where,
his love captured me.

Birds at the Altar

By Allison Moore Giles

"Even the sparrow finds a home, and the swallow a nest for herself, where she may lay her young, at your altars, O Lord of hosts,
my King and my God." Psalm 84:4

The whereabouts of nests, once hidden,
are now exposed and bare,
abandoned
on leafless twigs
against the grey sky,
signs that this palace was lately let
By full-throated kings.
But whither have they fled
On this rainy winter morning?

Even they know that You do not dwell
In houses of their own making,
But have fled beneath the shadow of
Your wings--
In the shadow of the Holy--
Where they, too, find contentment
When wintry wind rises
And showers fall,
And admire the drops of dew
You have strung like pearls round
Your altar gates
From whence they've flown
And from which they sang afar
Before they came to nestle
'neath the Throne.

Contemplations While Folding a Fitted Sheet

The ordering of
This shapeless mass
in my arms begins.
It flows in billows
from my clasped fingers.
I fold it over
against itself,
admiring the straight line that
appears along the fold,
Matching corners
Coaxed into place
And folded again,
A large sheet
Becoming small.
Is this how You felt
When You stretched out the sky
And tucked in its corners
Just so
Beneath the Bulges of islands
And the crevices of cliffs?
And did it fall softly at the borders
Your hands set in place,
Stretched out—
A thin, smooth covering
For the rippled, wrinkled waters
Underneath?

Breathe the Rain

By Ana Lauran

Something in its steady substance
renews me to
abide like the firm oak tree,
endure like the endless sea,
sustain like the resolute mountains.

Uniform, reliable, the white pond
of the sky pours like a river.
I've always wondered
if that pattern of translucent beads
is enchanted. How else,

if not through a miracle,
could it stop my anxieties in their tracks
and wash them away effortlessly?
I follow gravity tracing water drawings
on my window.

I spot last week's worry
in one of the silver droplets,
stable enough to glue to the glassy surface
and stay there until I can't remember
its origin anymore. I talk to Jesus.

The synchronized melody fills my mind:
calm, constant drops like
Beethoven's fingertips drip
the Moonlight Sonata on the ground,
hitting the black and white keys

of an ancient piano.
What a privilege it is to witness
the kiss between the earth
and the virgin rainwater! On those nights,
my soul leaves my body and hides

inside the core of the damp waterflakes.
My Lord offers me living water,
I am reminded as I breathe in.
Steadfast water,
unfaltering and unyielding.

Witnessing

It's these rugged trees that escort me in silence on morning walks
with pine-green limbs like eyelashes heavy with sleep.
They drag the sunrise on their foreheads and between
their toothless smiles, spots where
crumbling branches
have gone missing. As I drive to work,

it's these Western White Pines and Douglas-firs
that send their shadows to catch my back tires. We are lost
in a game of tag: me, the trees, and the lazy highway.
So I can't help but giggle then gaze
at their contour zigzagging the clumped backs
of hanging clouds,

while they wave like pretend aliens greeting in peace.
And it's these placid creatures
that follow me through the office window
—Grand-firs, Silver Pines, Western Hemlocks—
and I them; I envision their ruffled needles lethargically falling,
swinging with the wind, entangling
with the silhouettes of pine cones and squirrels and sporadic birds

in the microscopic distance. When I scurry back to my car,
the evening rain tickles my nose and stains my glasses.
There's this shimmer
through my bones and this skip in my heart
because it's them, still, wet and glorious like loyal Collies
awaiting to take me home.

Laid Bare

By Karyn Hunt

My last few golden brown leaves
wave from the tips of
my nearly bare branches;
clinging to their beauty
for as long as I can—
I am afraid to let them go,
to let them fall to join the rest
on the forest floor.
Once they are gone,
who will I be?
No lush green leaves
to hide birds' nests
and scampering squirrels;
no golden yellow leaves
to bring out smiles
from all who look at me;
Will I be enough
when my branches are bare?
When my gray-brown bark
is all that I wear?
Who will I be
with my beauty stripped away?
In this season of loss
I'll have nothing to display.

The Wind whispers an answer
as another leaf falls:
You are strong, you are mighty,
you are kind, you are brave,
you are home to many,

in other seasons you are shade;
your beauty lies within you,
your enough-ness does, as well—
underneath your gray-brown bark
is where they always dwell.
Three seasons of the year
you reveal what lies within,
but now's the time for rest,
for letting go of what has been.
With branches all laid bare
as you let your last leaf fall,
I still see who you truly are;
now rest—and await Spring's call.

Seeds

By Lindsey Gallant

For weeks I kept the seeds
in my pocket.

They mingled with cough drops
and soggy mittens,

showed up in spare change
and seemed to multiply.

They dropped out
in moments I most desired

poise, betraying my secret,
childlike wishes.

And then one blizzard
I crunched down the path

and heard, above the blast,
a lone but hopeful cheep

of solitary chickadee.
For such a storm as this

I reached into my treasure horde,
held my breath and one bare hand

to the sky, with a poise
only providence could supply.

Prismatic Color Theory: A Haibun

By Kelly Hellmuth

Why do we get to watch the sun rise? That delightful explosion of prismatic color theory, prompting copious questions of "what does this mean?" while we continue about our days? Is it to echo the vibrance of the dawn across our seemingly muted lives, igniting the atmosphere again and again in a burst of grace-filled glory? To be kaleidoscopic reflections of that God-hewn brilliance in a world living in black and white? It's possible. But maybe there's no why. Maybe there is no work to be done. Maybe we simply get to enjoy the Work that has already been completed. Maybe we just get to rest.

Coral clouds against
Waned midnight, stars fading, dim
Unveil "It is good"

Students Observe Nature

By Adam Ryan Barton

It's a fight to get them thinking, but their reticence is not personal.
They fight with their minds, enamored yet unsure until

a revelation, a thought that makes itself happen,
compels them to see the unspent world.

Can loving things be taught?
      The question is better framed as a showing.
      All things are a gallery of art—
      Yet we can touch their canvas,
      We can feel the grooves,
      We can feel their errors,
      Much less see them.

And on the walls, on the space between the works,
We find our reflections.
But we must do the work ourselves of observing the

white between majesty and majesty.

To see what's next, and to feel what's left behind,
Our eyes must be bored, our senses hushed but ready.

Then we will see where time resides,
That the spaces between what we see are themselves works.
They are ourselves because they are our turning minds.
But we ourselves must be there, if even for a second.

So as thought feels so much like confinement,
We affirm this prison as our greatest good.

I speak:

"You must sit and be stupid, stupefied at this carnal canvas, the air that pricks the skin, and the light that penetrates the eye, crediting what other creatures can't. It was before you came, and it will be after you are gone, and yet it is for you and your eyes, should you have the eyes to see. Only the stupid have the right to call themselves free. So be bored. Be stupid bored. It's about time we were."

Sea of Seven Colors

By Melissa Alvarado Sierra

Blue with a white necklace,
turquoise and lapis lazuli,
gold, silver, and bronze

dance upon the water,
capture the sun's divine gesture,
spill into an eternal rhythm.

Each wave a now,
each tide a song,
all together in prayer.

The fisherman's poem
is the poem of this sea,
of nets and lines,

filling with ancestral treasures—
and here they are,
vivid and unrestrained colors,

The vast canvas of the sea,
so beautiful and mysterious,
shining beneath the gaze of another blue.

A work of creation,
the palette of the great artist,
the seasoned air filled

with celestial laughter,
the splash of joy,
the seven colors of life.

Your Summer Windows

Bougainvilleas spill
over the white-washed wall,
wind lifts the curtains,
a whisper of salt and linen.
The hill slopes toward the sand,
where children chase the tide.

A small sail tilts,
alone in the warmth of noon.
It glides past the reef—
soft wake dissolving
in the secret of blue.

The heavenly disk turns bronze,
as waves hum against the rocks.
And in houses by the shore,
arms entangle,
feet swirl on the cool tile,
the laughter of glass.

By dawn, the sea is quiet,
sky wide, seafoam faint.
You open the windows,
air still fresh with night,
the summer comes in again.

Desire

By Kelli Sallman

What will I do to answer my heartache? Will I
step out of my shoes? Lace my feet with the
unknown?
        Yes.
                Forget the dead cat,
the bedrock of life is curiosity, a slipping
off of sandals on holy ground, wading into
waves, warm or cold, diving into the deep
end of your unfathomable mind. Whether
I lose my breath and drown or find a rhythm
of bobbing beneath the surface for sips of glory
before coming up for air, I must know you,
Lord. The deeper the pain, the weightier
the questions that drag me to your depths.
What will I experience before I expire?
Show me the majesty of sharks patrolling
these waters, the chaos of leviathan confined
to boundaries you set, and the life that
flourishes in the deep beyond humanity,
beyond all known parameters. These terrify
me—all. But let me inhale deeply the salt
of your tears. Let me taste and see what fills
these oceans. Let me feel you engulf me.
Let it be good. Let it be enough before I die.

When the Days of Your Sorrow Will Be Over

after Isaiah 60

Oh world! What sound creation sings
at summer's peak: Resplendent things
like frogs harrumphing in the creek,
their ruckus deep. Their echoes peek
through windows dim: Kids lie asleep
and dream of schoolless days gone by,
pockets full of croaking lullabies.

Under moonlit skies, proud crickets
rub their wings and firecracker leap
on legs like springs. Late lovers clink
stemmed bowls of wine; porcelain chimes
with spoon and tine. The many songs
upon the breeze blanket bare skin,
caress, and ease; dark days are done.

Come rise, dear sun! So dawns the morn
with gentle ache, its soul reborn.
Sound, pollinators! Buzzing bright,
day's symphonies transform the night.
Hearken, world, to the building roar:
Cicadas, climbing free, now soar,
abandoned shells hung on a tree.

Cottonwood

By Abigail Rainey

Let the sun wash your hair.

Listen for the roots
underfoot
like highways
carry drink surely
from the shore of a lake
to the leaves
of a tower
a great flowering
cottonwood—

the multitude flags
clapping to make
a sound like rain.

The wind has pressed
sand about
the base of her great trunk
carving a village of coves
where she has longed for and
hugged the earth.

Yes!
Look and see—

the sea of reasons
around you
like seasons circling
to remind you
the meaning and breathing
of Joy.

Go Find A Quiet Place

If you are able,
go find a quiet place.

Make some time
around sunset
then watch as the last gold of day
fades red then pink
and leaves everything around you
blushing.

Go stand under some trees
let your nose and fingers grow cold and
listen—

to God holding the earth
and His creatures therein
see Venus set to guard
the falling sky
that heavenly domain
lined with contrails
of a northbound jet.
Attend—

to gravity's silent pull
and the impossible flight
of insects at night.
Stay there, still,
acknowledge—

He is steadfast.
Go to the ebenezers
marking your days

mountainous love
throwing great cool shadows,
a rest for your desert past.
Cast—

Your sorrows on Him
Who hears all things and
bears all things

Wildflowers

By Julia McMullen

Like hands, they stretch
from grassy green beds,
boasting with a vibrant color
which applauds the morning.

They beckon me, my feet
comply, wandering among
their allure. Could they pull me
in, down into their stalks,
like sirens to a sailor?

I would not resist. Let me
be washed in the depth
of their beauty, sink into
the earth to feed
their morning songs.

Let me stay, sweet petals
resting on my eyes,
the wild, ancient fragrance
bathing me 'til I depart.

Detail of a grassy hill

A soft breeze whispers through
the blades, which dance with delight.

Above, song in flight fills the air.
Below, earth crawls and hops and hides.

Blessed are those sunshine-worshippers,
green and friendly, stretched and thin.

Blessed are the feet which tread there,
toes embraced and washed in dew.

Mine will remain there only moments
before the long sidewalk back home.

Let Me Not Forget

By Lauren Madsen

In mortal overwhelm
    faithfully spent
I remember Thee
yoked with me
transforming
    healing
        providing rest

First hint of worry
    future unknown
I remember Thee
past predicting present
listening
    soothing
        inspiring trust

With shattered spirit
    pain unforeseen
I remember Thee
in the garden, on the cross
pleading
    suffering
        forgiving all

At the casket
    grief unfathomed
I remember Thee
an empty tomb
speaking
    comforting
        breathing life

Through darkness I stumble
    anxiously blind
I remember Thee
Light of the World
guiding
    shining
        illuminating truth

In observing wanderers
    (sometimes it's me)
I remember Thee
Good Shepherd
rescuing
    leading
        gathering home

With each new day
    and possibility
I remember Thee
ever and always
strengthening
    sustaining
        remembering me

Maine

By Abigail Perez

Morning's gradient softly glows
through a singular skylight.
Denim jeans and navy Ked's tip-toe with delight
out into nature's evanescent glory.
Seventy steps descend down to a chestnut dock,
firs and balsam fragrancing the shore's quarry.
A lonely figure sits on a folding chair
loosely gripping a fishing pole,
the water the object of his stare.
Fledgling joined ancestral;
vague whispers exchanged in morn's mist
while a reclusive kestrel hovered above
a lobster boat, keeping his regular shift.
      A splash of surprise and what do they see?
Two porpoises at their feeding;
mother gently guiding her precious baby
out to greater sea for day's beginning.
And, as if on cue,
the sky turned an evermore intense pink hue.
      Crescendo of the cosmos!
Apollos unfolds out from night's shade,
his rays dappling Neptune's haven,
its impression a ripple over the moon's retrograde.
Russett squirrels race and chatter,
energized by electromagnetic matter;
their vibrancy almagating with the bluebird's singing.
      Wonders welling up in wide irises,
little blooms of inspiration desirous
grasped the tendrils of a sedentary brain
and wove it together as a loom would do with grain;
all orchestrated perfectly amongst the evergreens of Maine.

Counting Tov Teshura's

By Alexis Ragan

*Every good gift and every perfect gift is from above, and cometh down
from the Father of lights, with whom is no variableness, neither shadow
of turning. —James 1:17*

You give many of them, and often.
Every one of them, exemplary in nature.

Time and time again, we enjoy everything—yet

how often do we forget to fully embrace
the depth and beauty of their origin?

We consume, and then are glad.
Never used to not getting what
we think we must have.

But when we pause to place a magnifying glass
over each and every good gift You give, Father,

no matter how grand or delicate in size,
our wonder, our praise, EXPANDS.

Big Things—

The emergence of birth
and being made *Imago Dei*,
when God blew glitter across the galaxy
so we could see the night sky sparkle.
Wild rolling oceans populated
with colorful, busy sea life,
the delightful fruits of the Spirit.

and smaller things—

A hot continental breakfast,
newly birthed, fully fragranced roses,
A mug of roasted coffee with heavy cream
warming your cold hands, babies' laughs,
the smile of a stranger, warmth of sun on flesh.
And things we might not see good at first —

A sermon that pricks the heart,
the unexpected phone call,
the discipline of a parent...

these too are gifts.

Every present that is good and perfect
is showered upon us from the Father of brilliance,
in abundance, who's radiance stays steadfast
to bless us, never to shapeshift into darkness.

May our wonder and praise EXPAND!

Knowing the best gift is

and always will be
that crimson cloak over our souls.

The Divine Waits at Your Fingertips

I used to look only in places that glittered
with awe, monuments made to mirror
the Maker, mountains skyscraping towards
the heavens, but didn't dust make for man,
the pinnacle of creation, something holy?

Everywhere.

What I have found is
the divine exists everywhere,
not just in polished chapels.

It's not something hidden or held
directly in the light, it's in the neighbors
roses, fragrant in the dew of dawn,
it's in the grocer's smile, the one who made
today's food just for you, the students'
story, so eloquently written with words
that drip right off the page, or what about
the monarch, freshly hatched out of its cocoon
discovering for the first time this wild wide
open earth? What about grace? The kind
so undeserved it defies all human logic?

And sometimes there is nothing louder,
nothing more powerful than a whispered prayer.

Through The Cathedral Window

The stain glass is moving.
I tell you, angelic infant figures
are dancing in the encased pane
before my very child eyes!

I did not utter a word to the elders that day.
All I could do was stare and store it in soul.

No Skin-Deep Matter

you were sealed for the day of redemption —Ephesians 4:30

Fleeting ships and surface-level souvenirs
flick away into temporary landscapes

when I remind myself that
salvation still swims in my veins.

This is no skin-deep matter.
No tattoo quality promise

rendered "under one condition"—
Spirit cemented, forever contented,

food might suffice, or a friendly loan.
But you rest closer than muscle to bone.

Fiction

The Parable of the Storm

By Luke Waggoner

The prow cut through the dark, roiling sea with resolve. With each plunge and reemergence of the ship's bow, the salt spray stung me with a renewed chill. I looked up at the horizon, ever ominous with the deepening sapphire clouds amassing in our course.

"Is that it?"

"It would seem so," I replied, hoping to mask the trepidation in my own voice. I could feel my lieutenant's probing stare, desperate for consolation. I couldn't give it. The rumors of this passage were too well known, and yet virtually nothing was known about it definitively. No one had returned. Passage was either granted, in which case voyagers entered that long-sought blessed realm of no return, or they were refused and cast headlong into the deep for eternal rest. The binary finality of this approach forced a churning in my gut that mirrored the unsettled sea.

"Shall I give the order, sir?" My lieutenant's question hung in the charged air. Still staring into the growing gloom, I nodded solemnly. "Aye, captain." I heard him click across the paneled deck and shout down at the anxious crew.

"Heave forward!"

The crew sprang to their posts and assignments in a fierce and frenzied choreography. No one spoke, but everyone communicated: fear was in their eyes. A pall of doubt was palpable in their demeanor. Consternation forced rigidity into their movements, belying their feigned projections of courage. Their choreographed dance was more like sclerotic mimicry; a puppet show performed by novices.

My lieutenant returned to my side.

"Captain, what do you plan to do? I mean to say, what with the . . ."

"Yes, I know. The voice. To be honest, Lieutenant, I'm not entirely sure."

"I've heard it dissipates the very brain of any man who hears it." At this, I looked at him, annoyance faintly visible on my face.

"Surely you don't believe that, do you, Lieutenant?"

"Well, sir, I suppose it's far-fetched. But, who's to say definitively?"

"A fair point." I mulled this possibility, briefly, and then turned my focus back to what I believed. The storm would search me, would seek me out to know to what degree I am wanting. Then, passage would either be granted or denied. I was certain of little else.

As the gap between our ship and the dark clouds lessened, I swallowed hard. My gaze was fixed, but my mind was racing. Suddenly, I realized the darkness was enveloping us. I strained to see light through the clouds, but the only illumination was in the brief flashes of lightning followed quickly by sharp cracks of thunder. The strobing effect of the lightening coupled with the cripplingly loud thunder left me feeling unmoored, ill-equipped for whatever may transpire. I felt nausea grow in the pit of my stomach with each disorienting lurch of the ship in the dark, seething billows.

Then, I heard a rumbling, not of thunder. Rather, a purposeful, guttural utterance. The boat tossed and heaved violently. I grabbed the gunwale, narrowly avoiding being hurled into the foaming sea. I heard shouts of desperation on the deck below as the men sought security and shelter amid the storm. The sails were flapping helplessly in the tumult. The ship moaned and creaked, its integrity challenged by the exacting elements.

Suddenly, a sharp ray of light cut through the storm clouds, illuminating only the ship amid the dark waters. Like a child rocking a paper boat in a bucket of water, we were caught in the gaze of this light. The ray struck with a searching, demanding sensation. It pulled and pushed. It burned and cooled. Unable to bear the intensity of this beam, I finally cried out, "What is it? What do you require of me?"

Then a voice came out of the whirlwind and said, "By what right do you come here?"

I puzzled at the question. "Well, no right. I have none."

"Then why would I let you pass?"

Again, I puzzled. I could think of no reason why I should be allowed into the blessed realm. Why had I not considered this question? Why had I not composed a compelling reason for my admittance? Then I realized with dread and deep sadness, I had none. I stood despondent for a moment, looking into the dark cauldron of turmoil all around me. I didn't know what to say. In sincere desperation, I looked up and uttered, "I'm not sure you should, but by your mercy."

Another deep groan amid the storm. And with that, the waters calmed. The light that pierced that dark place spread, casting out the clouds. As the sky cleared, the sun shone down with a cleansing light. I felt renewal. Life welled up within me. I closed my eyes and basked in the warmth of that moment. And when I opened my eyes and stared out at the horizon, there, I beheld the blessed realm.

It Never Gets Old

By Rachael Maddox

The angel lingers, watching.

A man sits alone in the back pew of a dark church. His shoulders are hunched, his hands clasped together, not in confidence but in something fragile—uncertainty, hesitation, the final vestiges of resistance. The angel sees the weight pressing on him, the years of doubt, the unanswered questions, the scars of disappointment that have hardened his heart.

And yet, he is here.

The angel has seen empires rise and fall. He has witnessed the Red Sea part, felt the tremble of the earth at the moment of resurrection, beheld the splendor of the Lamb upon His throne.

The angel has stood at the threshold of eternity, beheld the birth of stars, and witnessed the breaking of the curse upon the world.

The angel has seen altars built and temples crumble. He has watched the great revivals and the quiet conversions, the mighty proclamations and the whispered confessions. But this moment—this small, trembling moment—stills him.

It never gets old.

The man exhales, his lips barely moving. The prayer is quiet, almost imperceptible. A breath of surrender. The words are raw, unpolished, nearly broken—

"I believe."

Heaven stills.

The angel leans in, hearing what the man cannot—the voice of the King whispering his name, claiming him as His own.

The man does not know that all of heaven has been waiting for this moment. He does not see the unseen realm trembling with anticipation. He does not know that, in this solitary moment of surrender, the gates of eternity are opening to receive him.

And then—

The eruption. A deafening roar. The triumphant cry of a kingdom welcoming a prodigal home. The heavens blaze with joy, the King Himself rejoicing over the one who was lost and is now found.

The man lifts his head, unaware of the holy celebration. He only knows that, for the first time, the weight has lifted. A tear escapes.

The angel smiles.

Heaven is watching. And heaven is in awe.

The Banyan Tree

By Meredith Chester

"However many you'd like," said the stall attendant, resting his hands on the counter.

The little girl stood on her tiptoes, taking in the colors of the small plastic frogs which filled the large jar in front of her. Green seemed the obvious first choice, as it's the color one might most associate with a frog. For her, no image or setting or painting was complete without a shade of green.

"You don't have to pick just one. Take however many you'd like, just not all." The stall attendant glanced around the alleyway. There was no line, but he seemed anxious to send her on her way.

She looked up at his bronze skin, his graying stubble, and his leathery neck, then looked away quickly when his dark eyes met hers. She was used to the impatience of adults, but this man didn't broadcast his quite as loudly as others. She wanted to stay a while and consider the plastic frogs. For her, that was the real prize. She'd tossed eight balls and knocked over eight bottles, not to rush to the next stall, but to stand up close to the beautiful jar. The idea that her presence should impede his solitude seemed at first impossible to her, but she realized he was obligated to remain attentive for as long as she stood there.

At the end of the alley near the river, past the shops and stalls, stood a banyan tree as big as a house. The thought of exploring its hollows and branches beckoned her with sudden, irresistible urgency. She wondered with delight how the frogs might look nestled safely into the crevices of its enormous trunk and how high up she might be able to place them in its branches. Eagerly she began her selections, picking out most of the greens, carefully leaving a few behind for the benefit of the jar's aesthetic. She took some violets, yellows, blues, and magentas as well. With their candy colors, molded lines, and tiny flaps of melted extra plastic hanging from their edges, they were not realistic or well-crafted, but she had a hunch their rough imperfections would make them cling well to the grooves and safety of the banyan. She would find out.

The stall attendant sighed as he watched the little girl march with purpose up the alley toward the river, clutching her bag of prize frogs. He thought for a moment about her remarkable throwing accuracy and her choice of many plastic frogs over a large stuffed bear, but he quickly lost the thought as he sat back down in his chair in front of the fan and turned the radio up.

Running a stall in a river festival was brutal in the subtropical heat, but he liked having time to think. Today, he also had time to record the appearance of a cumulonimbus cloud at 12:53pm in the tiny logbook which he kept in his shirt pocket. This was a game he'd played with his daughter when she was young—a game which he still carried on, alone.

He tilted his head back in his chair and thought. The next day he'd work as a fishing guide. For years, he'd freelanced as a crew member on a charter boat shuttling tourists on a journey notorious this time of year for unpredictable weather patterns and boating conditions. When she was little, his trips made his daughter nervous about her father's safety. He could still hear her asking repeatedly about the weather. To prove his own attentiveness and to cultivate hers, he'd bought her a *Field Guide to Weather* by the National Audubon Society and proposed that they record the types of clouds and weather events they each observed throughout the day. Comparing logs at bedtime seemed to ease her anxiety. Continuing his own log eased his now.

He glanced at the jar several times, then leaned forward and picked out one of the frogs. He turned it over in his hands, feeling the grooves of the plastic. "Blessed is the one whose delight is in the law of the Lord . . . " came a deep, crackling voice over the radio. He studied the frog's crudely constructed form, lost in his thoughts. " . . . that person is like a tree planted by streams of water . . . " The mention of water conjured up visions of angry waves crashing against him during storms, not of steadfast streams. He wiped his forehead. He wasn't afraid of the Gulf, but anxiety still pulled him in different directions like a receding wave pulls loads of seashells away from the land, only to launch them forward again in a crashing spray. He began to imagine being "planted" by the same God who designed the tides to change.

"Hello! How much to play?" A woman pulled a little boy up to the counter. Startled, he rose from his chair.

The channel coastlines were bordered by thick mangroves, but the river's edges were composed of only mud and rocks. After his shift, the stall attendant walked along the river. The single cumulonimbus cloud had multiplied into glorious plumes of color with the setting sun. For a moment, his heart ached, but he quickly pulled out his logbook and entered a description: "6:51pm, multiple layers of cumulonimbus clouds towering over the river, dark purple on the bottoms, gold and pink and white to the tops." He paused, then suddenly added, "They look like mountains!" Returning the logbook to his shirt pocket, he spotted one of the green plastic frogs from his stall on the ground. He picked it up thoughtfully and tucked it safely into his pocket behind the logbook. Then he raised his face toward the cascades of color in the sky. "Help me, God," he breathed. A great white egret rested in the banyan tree and the leaves moved softly in the breeze.

No Matter the Mountain or Valley, He is with Us

by Taylor Blayse

An Allegory Inspired by Psalms 23:1-4

The sand was warm between her toes. As soon as she stepped foot onto the beach, the door behind her shut, and the Valley vanished with it. Milo the cat was by her side. She felt a sense of peace, even though the chaos from what had just happened still stirred in her heart. Feelings from the old door still lingered. She felt ashamed of this grief that seemed to follow her everywhere she went.

"Just because you have stepped through this new door doesn't mean the hurt from the last one won't follow you. I sense more in your heart. There is bitterness and anger. That's okay. You were strong enough to close that door and enter this one. I'm proud of you." Milo said.

Dahlia wept.

Milo curled up in her lap and purred strongly. She was walking through the lands of grief. She had just experienced the first trial: letting the door close on something you love. Now she was one step closer to everything God had planned for her.

"You are following Him. It's not always easy, but it is always worth it. Sometimes, there's a lot you'll have to let go. But I promise you, what you gain will be so much greater than what you've left behind."

"I just don't understand it," Dahlia began. "I'm grieving; but at the same time, I don't think I've ever felt this much peace. How can that be?"

"You're learning that He *is* peace. And because of this, He is planted in your heart now. He always was, but you didn't always know it. He is peace in the midst of chaos. Not in front of you, not behind you, but in the midst of the mess in your heart. He is our rock and our strength. You're learning that piece by piece. And He is patient and loving as you do."

Dahlia wasn't sure what to say. Before she had experienced the Valley of the Doors, where she watched several of them close in front of her, she couldn't grasp the concept of letting something or someone you love go. How could anyone bear it?

But Dahlia remembered the many doors that had been opened after she had let the others close. There was a wave of peace in her heart as she slowly accepted these things.

"Milo, you are the most loyal friend I've ever had."

They sat there together, soaking up the sunshine and enjoying the sand. It was nice for them both to rest after a trial as difficult as the Valley of the Doors. But Dahlia knew more was coming.

"See that cliff over there?" Milo asked. "We're going to climb to the very top of it. But I should caution you, Dahlia. I will be with you as we journey up the hill, but once we arrive, I must leave you again."

"But why?" Dahlia asked, feeling the tears fighting to let loose from her eyes once more.

"It is another part of the journey that you must learn to face alone. But please don't fear, you are never alone. He is always with you. It will all make sense when it arrives, I promise," Milo reassured her.

Dahlia trusted her dear friend.

They abandoned their resting place on the beach and began to walk in the sand along the sea. The sound of the waves lapping against the shore gave Dahlia a sense that everything would be okay. She even smiled to herself as she walked.

As they neared the edge of the mountain, Dahlia's heart grew fearful. She knew uncertainty lay just around the bend.

The dreadful mountain was now right at their feet. They peered up at it together.

"Ready?" Milo asked.

"No . . . but I know I can do it," Dahlia replied.

"That's the spirit!" Milo exclaimed.

They began. There was a nice path laid out for them at first, and the land was flat. It was easier to navigate than she thought.

Unfortunately, that didn't last long. The mountain began to grow steeper by the minute. Dahlia had to use her hands to grab onto rocks and tree limbs. She feared she would slip and fall all the way back down.

Breathless, tired, and weary, Dahlia continued to climb with Milo at her side. As she reached out her hand to grab hold of a sturdy rock, something beautiful and purple caught her eye. She realized it was not just an exquisite flower—it had a face.

"Hello, dear!" The flower exclaimed.

"Umm . . . hi there."

"I'm Dolores. You must be Dahlia. I'm delighted to meet you, dear."

Dahlia took in her surroundings. She realized, suddenly, that Dolores was the only piece of color on this mountain. Everything was black and white. She looked at Milo, whose orange fur had shifted to dark gray. Even her hands had changed. But Dolores remained bright.

"What happened to the color?" Dahlia asked.

"That happens on this mountain, dear. I'm afraid you're nearing your next trial. The closer you get, the less color you see. But don't fret, it will return."

"Why are you still purple?"

"Because I am a gift from Him. He planted me here ahead of time, with great care, knowing that you would travel up this mountain as you healed your heart. I'm here to serve as a gentle reminder that He has not forgotten you. He asks if you will accept this gift?"

Dahlia's eyes began to well up with tears. An overwhelming feeling of love washed over her entire body.

"Of course I will," She said.

Dolores smiled brightly. She urged Dahlia to pluck her away from the rocks where she was growing. She wanted to join Dahlia now—to serve as a constant reminder of His thoughtfulness and love. Dahlia gently plucked her and placed her lovingly into the side pocket of her backpack. Dolores settled into the new dirt.

A gift from the One who held her heart—who always would, no matter life's trials.

A Solitary Mite

By Liz Jakimow

*For all these out of their abundance have put in offerings for God, but
she out of her poverty put in all the livelihood that she had. (Luke 21:4)*

One mite. A solitary mite. I clench it tightly in my hands,
hoping no one will see it. It is not enough for the temple treasury.
But it is all I have. One mite. It is everything I own in the world.

I take a peek through my clenched fingers, hoping it has
somehow miraculously increased. But no. It is still the one mite.
A solitary mite.

Maybe I shouldn't put this in. People will see me. They will
laugh at me. It looks pitiful. Puny. Worthless. They will think that
I am too stingy to put in a greater amount. Either that, or they
will guess that I am poor.

Besides, what is one mite in the temple treasury? Compared
to all the other larger amounts being put in, it is like a drop in
the ocean, a grain of sand on the beach, a feather amongst a flock
of birds. A solitary mite in the temple treasury. It won't do any
good. God doesn't need it. It's not like it's going to be useful. I
can't see them saying, "I'm so glad this widow put in her mite.
Otherwise, we'd never survive."

Perhaps I should keep it. I give this away, and then I have
nothing. One mite may not mean a lot to the temple, but it means
something to me.

Yes. It does mean something to me. It means something to me
to give. Despite the fact that it's all I have, despite the fact that it
will not help the temple, it helps me to know that I have given. It
may be small. But it is something. That means something to me.

I unclench my fingers and let the mite drop into the temple
treasury. I glance around furtively, hoping no one has seen me. I
should be so lucky. Jesus is there and, not only has he seen me, but
he is pointing me out to his disciples.

Great, I think. *Not only have I given away all that I possess, but I am now to be ridiculed for not giving enough.* But no. It appears not. For despite the distance, I can hear his words.

"I tell you the truth," he says. "This poor widow has put more into the treasury than all the others. They all gave out of their wealth; but she, out of her poverty, put in everything—all she had to live on."

True enough. It doesn't help me now, though. For now, I have nothing, and how shall I eat? Already, I am growing dizzy for I have not eaten in days. I need food, and I have no money to buy any. So I gave more than all the others. So I gave everything, all that I had to live on. What does that help me? And in the end, what does it help God? God will not benefit from my solitary mite.

I feel faint. I need to sit down. The room starts to swim around me. I look over at Jesus and see the words he has just spoken, the words about me, written in a book. Some kind of hallucination. I shake my head, but it doesn't disappear. Now I see people reading those words. Ghostly forms of people. Not real people. Not people here in the temple. But other people. From the future, maybe. They read his words, and then they give the temple treasury money. Lots of money. Huge amounts of money. It keeps coming and coming and coming. More money than I have ever seen before. They read the words and then they give.

The ghostly figures disappear. The room becomes solid again. Strange imaginings from lack of food? But it felt so real. It wasn't, though. Nothing but a starving body affecting a suggestible mind. I start to walk outside. As I walk past Jesus, he seems as though he is still talking to his disciples. But I hear some words addressed only to me.

"They will give because of you," he says. "Throughout the ages, many people will give money because of what you just did. Your solitary mite made a wealth of difference."

I stare at Jesus, but he still talks to his disciples. Was it all in my mind? Of course, it was. Silly, hungry woman that I am. Making up things.

On the way home, I keep my eyes open for anything that I can eat. Grass, maybe. How would that taste? Dead bugs. No, it's against God's laws. Although locusts are okay. I wonder how easy they are to catch.

Searching around, I see something on the ground that I wouldn't usually see. I come closer and find that it is a mite. A solitary mite. What do you know? A mite isn't much, but at least I'm no worse off than I was this morning. Then I spot another one, some distance from the first. I pick it up and add it to the first. Two mites. I keep walking. There is another mite. Three mites. By the time I get home, I have found and picked up ten mites. All of them were found by themselves. A solitary mite, plus a solitary mite, plus a solitary mite, plus seven other solitary mites, equals ten mites. Still not a fortune. But enough.

Going Home

By Henry Lewis

It was frigid darkness and dead cold. Eye-freezing frigid. A night inhospitable to life.

The wind drove hard from the west, icy snow pelting everything, pounding without end in a steady, thrashing gale. There was no hope of warmth. It was minus 30 Fahrenheit, extremely dangerous. The only sound of howling darkness pervaded by the desperate rasping breath of cold death.

Bob did not care, not really. He had seen too many blizzards in his time.

It is just a Minnesota winter, he had thought as he maneuvered his vehicle through the blindness, his gloved hands steady on the wheel, glazed eyes fixed on pulsing white snow and ice crystals fragmenting and accumulating on the edges of the windshield and wipers. But now he could barely perceive a road or an intersection or anything in the raging white. This was *an honest-to-god stunner*—a true blizzard—one that happened maybe once or twice in as many decades. This was a night he could talk about when he was old and worn out, and all he had left was to tell stories. He smiled at the thought, rubbing his eyes to relieve the strain. This kind of storm could weary a person. Why, he had seen it all on his nightly patrols, he had seen everything. There were no surprises anymore.

The blizzard had descended with an almost catastrophic strength, exerting its frozen muscle on the metro area, and left the entire city cold to the bone. Bob's hands gripped the wheel of his vehicle more tightly as he peered blindly into night, helpless in a curtain of driving snow and deafening wind.

The blinding white sheared the dark night with a violence, howling in strength, driven parallel in his bright headlights. Bob stared into the madness, eyes fixed on the road before him, now become an imagined thing, the dulling pound of wind and snow and unrelenting roar of naked strength.

If he were honest, it took all his capacity to see the road at all. On a night like this, things were not always what they appeared. A storm could play tricks on you, give you a fiction for a truth. What might seem a driveway was an intersection, and what might seem like a trash can or a bush may become a person.

No, wait, what was that? A person? Not tonight, not in this storm. No, it was a bush or something, had to be. But no, it was walking now, walking slowly, yes walking, almost sauntering it was. He could not believe his eyes. What was this?

Bob slowly maneuvered his patrol vehicle up to the person and stepped out into the unforgiving wind. It was too cold to get out. Nobody should be out tonight, not in this weather. A person could freeze to death in little time. He had to do something.

With his collar turned up and his head bent into the cold, Bob made his way to the person. They had stopped and turned. It was a bundled-up woman in an overcoat that nearly reached the ground. A very elderly woman with calm eyes. Bob was immediately taken with her eyes. Not a care in this world. She seemed unconcerned by the harsh and terrible night.

"Can I help you?" He shouted in the wind.

"I'm going home," she replied calmly, and then she smiled.

"I can help, I'm an officer, I can take you home."

Bob spoke hurriedly. The cold was too much. He had to get this woman into his vehicle, where it was warm and safe. She looked at him, then his vehicle, and without a word, slowly walked to the passenger door. He got her seated and closed the door against the threat and storm. When he climbed back into the vehicle, he could feel warmth returning to his face and hands, his own body giving a sudden tremor as it absorbed warmth. There was nothing to compare to this extreme temperature and the violence of the night. It was the darkest of nights and searing cold.

The woman's name was Helen. She was ninety-two.

Their conversation was almost cordial. She seemed an eminently pleasant woman. Bob could be gruff and intimidating at times. As an officer, he had seen life's raw underbelly, and it had hardened him over the years. Yet underneath, his heart was kind, and he looked for the good of people. He hoped for it. With

Helen, there was no need to hope. She was a treasure. A sweet old woman that he had come to care for in an instant. He was glad he had found her and glad he could help.

"Where do you live, Helen?"

"Sheltering Arms," Helen paused. "I am going home, you know."

"That's right Helen", Bob's voice gentle, "I'm taking you home."

And they drove on into a night where there was no comfort.

Helen had been walking a good distance from the Sheltering Arms home, and Bob could not reconcile this. Just casually walking along like she had been, as if it were a perfect spring day and new life coming to be all around you. Yet it was not. It was bitter cold and too severe for any living thing at all. And surely not for a fragile aging flower such as Helen. She needed care, and how did she get so far from home?

Helen interrupted his thoughts.

"I have looked for it all my life, waited for it, if you want to know."

And then she was silent once again, seated as she was in her radiant calm.

In the warmth, violent gusts of blizzard white rocked the vehicle as it slowly made its way along.

It struck Bob that she was disconnected from the harsh realities around her, living in quiet anticipation of something, a someone, maybe, perhaps a husband or one of her children, he did not know. But she clearly did not grasp the imminent danger in the night, she all wrapped up like she was in her long overcoat and disarming calm, perilously unaware of the deadly storm. He had seen other older people gradually lose touch with their reality. And here was sweet Helen blissfully unaware of her treacherous situation, living in simple expectation of some good. And who would not want some good, why, even Bob wanted for good.

He had to ask. "What are you waiting for, Helen?"

"Home. My home, Bob." She looked out the windows and then her gaze fell to her lap as she said, "I was made for something finer, made for the good land, you know. I have waited a lifetime, and it is time now to go home. I am tired. It is time."

And she was silent then.

The good land. Bob could feel the weight of her words. He had often longed deeply for such a world. He had seen too much violence and evil, had seen too many friends' lives dissolve into despair and death from the hideous things they had seen, the endless perversions of man. Life as an officer had exposed him to such tragedy and unimaginable horrors. And how do you carry the weight, how do you bear the evil you have known? Unlike so many friends, he had found redemption and release. Bob could hear the words now, for they were always there.

Come to me, all who labor and are heavy laden, and I will give you rest.

And, yes, he had come, he had laid his burdens down, and he had found rest. Was this what Helen was talking about, was this the good land she aspired to and longed for?

"Well, I know it all comes good at the last," she said and sighed as she looked out the window at the danger of the world, "Things are not what they appear, Bob. I have come to see that in my life, not what they appear at all."

Bob had wondered if Helen was oblivious of her surroundings, lost in some tangled dementia, but no. She saw the dark night and the terrible wind and snow. She comprehended it all, and yet she was at rest. *Radiant almost*, he thought. She was waiting, that was all, waiting for her passage home, for she had said it was time.

And he felt for her, felt her longing, for he felt it too. At times, the world just wore you down, and you knew your frailty in it all, and the darkness just too much to bear. And what was *home* after all? He had felt God's comfort and redemption breaking into his own personal hell, had felt the clean release and calm. And sweet Helen at ninety-two years of age? Why, she had simply grown weary, her long journey nearing its end. She was hearing the song of the good land, of being home at long last, and how could she not?

It was then that Helen spoke in words softly spoken, her voice unwavering.

"Lord, you have been our dwelling place in all generations. Before the mountains were brought forth, or ever you had formed the earth and the world, from everlasting to everlasting you are God."

And she sighed once again, smiled, and said, "Home, Bob, it is the best place to be."

In the past, Bob had not considered *the Lord* as something of any practical use. His own struggles had changed all that. These days, he would often contemplate his life with the Lord. He understood Helen's words perfectly. She had spoken with a clear voice in this darkest of nights. He had found her wandering, out on a cold, forbidden night, and he was bringing her home, or so he had thought. But things are not what they appear. Not in this world.

Helen's thin, frail hands lay bare and fragile in her lap as she sat quietly in the passenger seat. There was no sense of urgency or worry, only her disarming calm, a tranquility on the threshold of eternity.

Then Helen spoke. "Thank you for taking me home. I have waited a good long while for it, waited all my life."

He rolled his vehicle to a stop to ascertain where the Sheltering Arms parking lot entry was. Nothing was obvious. The driving snow made it difficult to see anything at all. In a few moments, he advanced his vehicle forward, slowly turned, and moved cautiously into the lot. The other vehicles were parked haphazardly as people had returned in the disorienting night. Bob brought his vehicle to the front entry and stopped. He left the engine running. They needed the warmth.

"Well, here we are, Helen. Home," Bob spoke quietly, for he knew it was not the destination she so deeply longed for.

Helen glanced through the ice-crusted glass at the entry of the Sheltering Arms. The lobby was brightly lit and welcoming.

"Bob, I am going home," she said, "not Sheltering Arms. I am going home."

With that, she turned and looked peacefully once again through the windshield and the storm that raged beyond the glass. Bob could not simply drop her off without a word, he had to say something. He spoke gently.

"My mission tonight, Helen, is to bring you this far on your journey. I am not sure when it will continue, but perhaps it will not be long, and another will help you on your way."

Bob helped Helen from his vehicle.

He put his big arms around sweet Helen, and she leaned into his tenderness and warmth as they walked together into Sheltering Arms.

In the days following, Bob frequently thought of Helen. And when he thought of her, he imagined she had made her way home at last, and was just then casually walking along as if it were a perfect spring day and new life coming to be all around, for her new life was coming, and it was no longer a fiction but a truth.

Nonfiction

Remember to Look out the Windows

by Isabel Chenot

I wore myself out with errands yesterday. So today, I had to sit on the couch with a cup of tea and watch the leaves shiver in spats of wind. I saw a nimbus flutter around a bird, and a long, branched shadow needle along the fence slats, knitting up light.

In one of my favorite Spanish poems ("El fantasmo y yo"), Amado Nervo compares our five senses to "cinco ventanitas" or "five little windows". These little windows are set in a tower—the human body—that imprisons the soul. C. S. Lewis also wrote a poem about our senses, and he used similar imagery of being guarded in an interior. But in Lewis' poem ("On Being Human"), the interior is "charmed" and being guarded spares us from "imminent death": We could not bear the "dazzling edge of beauty unsheathed." Or, as God put it to Moses: we cannot see His face and live. The barriers between our frangibility and an utterly sharp beauty allow us to exist. Lewis is not trying to wrangle his soul through to the other side of his body—he is reveling in the interior. Because our sense perceptions not only sheathe an unbearable encounter with God's beauty, they translate His whispers. The angels, from angles of limpid intelligence, apprehend trees in ways we cannot fathom, but they have no skin: they do not feel the edge of a tree's shadow where it fissures sunlight. That is one of God's secrets. The angels "have no nose"—they cannot smell an apple blossom. Such "pleasure and the pang" are only experienced in here, in this "tiny parlor of the brain"—a five-little-windowed privacy we share with our Maker, our incarnate Redeemer.

But I forget to look out the windows. I get busy, glued to a screen, stuck on a blind (circular) track of anxiety. I shutter the windows and seal myself in. I grope around my mind in the dark, and a black hole vacuums up all the air. Because in shuttered-up space, someone other than God whispers. And it's easy to yield to that whisper, to its furtive insistence that I have not been given what I need. That I don't have enough. God isn't giving me enough.

But God is always plying infinity, huge and lavish, against my shutters. Eternally barbed and dazzling out there—homelike, and familiar in here. Streaks of lamplight, dawn colors, glowing slats, and blowing shadows of leaves. Threads of song, shining letters on spines of books, the reflective grain of a table.

When I do remember to open my senses, to look out, I am flooded with so much more than I know how to take in. I can smell Spring. Send my own shadow wavering through sunshine, feel the shudder a dove's wing. And I understand secrets. My little imprisonment runs over.

Open your eyes. Receive your sight. Taste and see that the Lord is good.

Restore the Wonder

By Jana Carlson

We crest the last foothill on our drive out of the city, heading toward Canada's majestic Rocky Mountains. Over a cerulean canvas, the sunrise paints the sky with fusions of apricot and fuchsia. Stately pines mount the slate ridges ahead, pointing to the whipped cream peaks adorning the mountain range. In the valley below, the wheat fields ripple in the golden light of the dawn.

This spectacular view looks the same yet different every time, depending on the weather and the time of day. No matter what, it moves me to worship. "Wow," I whisper. My husband chuckles. "You say that every time we make this drive!" He's right. But I can't help myself. Even when I anticipate this moment and make a mental note to keep my thoughts to myself, my awe spills out of my mouth like popping corn on a hot stove, completely uncontainable.

We used to live in a valley nestled between the mountains we're visiting today, surrounded by those towering rocky summits. Houseguests often asked me if I got bored of the view. They thought I might become immune to the splendor of the setting, but I didn't. How could anyone overlook the magnificence of this place? To me, it's unthinkable.

They say familiarity breeds contempt—we become careless about people, situations, or even dazzling landscapes we know well. I can't say it's been the case with this particular view, but it occurs to me that this is sometimes true of other areas of my life. When I hear the gospel message in church every week, I can lose my appreciation of it and become careless with my wonder. I forget the magnitude of what Christ has done for us and skim the passages about his death and resurrection, reading on autopilot, relieved when I get to the end of the chapter or book as though I've finally arrived at my destination.

How can I retain my wonder at the glorious gospel truth? When I arrive at the accounts of Jesus' death and resurrection in my Bible reading, I want to meditate on the miracle of it like I did the first time. Faced with the implications of the gospel in books like Romans and Ephesians, I want my heart to stir with praise and gratitude for all the riches available to us in Christ Jesus, no matter how often I read these precious passages.

So, I pray with David, "Restore to me the joy of your salvation" (Ps. 51:12 ESV). *Restore the wonder.*

My husband and I celebrated 26 years of marriage last year. Together for more than half our lives, "familiarity" seems to understate the depth of our knowledge about each other. During our morning routine last week, we seamlessly moved around the kitchen like accomplished dancers in a well-choreographed production. I grabbed the coffee pot, he handed me a mug; as he sat at the table, I slid him a plate with steaming, buttery toast. All the while, we chattered about everything from politics to pastry.

Caught up in our bustle and banter, I made a flippant remark, expecting my husband to respond with a smirk and a self-deprecating comment before heading out the door. But he surprised me with the most gentle and gracious correction.

I stood at the window watching him prepare to leave for work, and he looked up, smiled, and nodded before driving off. Our earlier exchange replayed in my mind, followed by flashbacks of similar moments spanning over two decades—my thoughtless comments, followed by my husband's patient responses. In some scenes, he overlooked my offense; in others, his kindness and subtlety nudged me toward the realization of my foolishness.

How had I missed this? All these years, he had put up with my disrespectful dialogue without condemnation. More than that, his devotion, affection, and attention have been generous, and I realize now, far beyond what I deserve. Humbled, I marvel at this man I married and wonder at his love for me.

Suddenly, I understand the key to keeping a sense of wonder about the gospel: humility. I must remember who I am without Christ—a depraved sinner without hope and destined for an eternity in hell. My greatest qualities, my most selfless good deeds, and my best moral intentions still fall far short of God's holy standard.

Still, he loves me. While I was yet a sinner, Christ died for me (Rom. 5:8). His sacrifice and my sinfulness—an outrageous contrast. What marvelous grace!

As we arrive again at the topmost hill on the highway, I behold that breathtaking display of God's masterful creation, full of wonder that never grows old, and worship anew with Psalm 8:

"O Lord, our Lord,
   how majestic is your name in all the earth!
You have set your glory above the heavens...
When I look at your heavens, the work of your fingers,
   the moon and the stars, which you have set in place,
what is man that you are mindful of him,
   and the son of man that you care for him?
Yet you have made him a little lower than the heavenly beings
   and crowned him with glory and honor...
O Lord, our Lord,
   how majestic is your name in all the earth! (Ps. 8:1, 3–5, 9 ESV).

The Crumb in the Sky

By Kris Ann Valdez

"The moon is a crumb in the sky," my five-year-old informs me from the creaking patio glider where she sits, rocking and staring at the moon on this dusky evening. "It will get smaller and smaller and then it'll disappear."

"Tell me," I say, "what happens after the moon disappears?"

"Oh," she says, pressing her hands together, "don't worry, it always comes back."

She turns and beams at me, her thin face half-lit by the glowing coach light.

I'm certain she believes this is her discovery—as if no one else has ever considered the moon's mysterious ways.

I feign illumination. "Thank you for teaching me that."

"You're welcome."

Someday, I will inform her of the moon phases, she will read it in a book, or a know-it-all at school will tell her. But tonight, I protect this naivety, to let her shoot her ideas, bright and burning as a Borealis, into the world. To believe she is a keeper of knowledge, the key tucked into the pocket of her favorite swirly dress. No one can snatch it from her as surely as the stars cannot be plucked from the sky. Belief in the wondrous and mysterious is her childhood right.

When her older brother was four, he called the moon La Luna, as if they were old friends.

"Is she really made of cheese?" he asked one day when we'd finished a picture book.

"No," I said," La Luna is made of rocks and metal. But if she were cheese, I'd like her to be mozzarella."

"That's a joke," he pointed out.

"Yes, it is," I said, my heart waxing and waning.

Now the boy who believed the moon could be cheese is ten. Too old to believe made-up stories of moons, faeries, or monsters.

If he were sitting on the front porch with us now, he'd pro-test, "That's not true, VV! It's not a crumb!" for he is ever the guarder of facts, slayer of fiction.

Perhaps, it is my fault. I bought him too many nonfiction picture books—and none ever described the lunar cycles in terms of crumbs.

Perhaps it is not my fault. What mother desires her child to outgrow her as he rounds into manhood, leaving only a sliver of the boy behind?

Ah, a mother's heart. Always eager for the future, always yearning for the past. Such a nostalgic little organ.

Wasn't it only yesterday I birthed the little girl rocking next to me?

While the moon is not a crumb, like the last crispy bits left in a potato chip bag to be swallowed by the night sky, nor is the young crumb rocking in a creaky chair, red boots plastered on her feet, a moon.

Instead, she will grow into a fullness that can never wane again.

Tonight, I wish children were moons.

Jesus Is in the Kitchen

A Slice of Life Reflection on Jesus, Emmanuel—
God with Us

by Amandalea Rodriguez Noel

It was evening as the four of us sat around the table eating dinner. Through the window, night began trickling in as the Advent candles flickered amidst the warm glow of the Christmas tree. Underneath my daughter's chair lay scattered grains of rice—customary for a two-year-old. Silvery dots sprinkled the scratched glass where my son, Averyn, had spilled his milk.

We were talking about usual things. Averyn was spouting on about some gadget or trinket he wanted for Christmas. My husband, in between bites of food, shared about his day, as he fed our daughter, Emerie, who wiggled in her seat and playfully slid her bowl back and forth against the table.

Our conversation was light and inconsequential until my little two-bit, seated in a chair far too large for her tiny frame, raised her hands, amidst the spilled milk, clattering bowl, and flickering candles, and declared, "Jesus in the kitchen."

At first, I wasn't confident I was hearing her correctly. Surely, she wasn't talking about *Jesus* being in our kitchen, so I asked her to say it again. Then again. Finally, I echoed her words as a question: "Jesus is in the kitchen?"

"Yes," she said emphatically, reciting the words over and over.

My husband's eyes widened with surprise and delight. Averyn giggled while I kept probing, hoping she'd offer an explanation. She didn't. All I was gonna get was that simple, cryptic statement.

What she saw or what she meant—I didn't know. After the kids were put to bed, as I wiped the counter and cleared the dishes, her words lingered in the air, trailing the quiet musings of my mind. *Jesus is in the kitchen.* Loading the plates in the dishwasher, I smiled to myself—*of course he is.* Certainly, he is present here in the heart of our home, in the middle of our family, among the mess and loveliness that make up the moments of our lives.

He's in the piles of laundry and crumbs on the floor. He's present in every chore, even every diaper change.

He's also in the most intimate of spaces—the bedroom, the bathroom—vulnerable places, where we are afraid to invite him inside. And if we dared to look, we would see him in the attic, amongst the cobwebs and boxes that have been cast aside and neglected. He's there and has not forgotten.

Whether he's waiting between the damp walls of the basement, or permeating a cool autumn breeze, he longs to meet us in the murky and marvelous minutes of our daily lives.

Because that is just like our God, the one who made himself known in the lowliest of circumstances: a king born in a stable, crowned upon a cross. He's still revealing himself today, most notably in our joy and in our pain, but often he's speaking through mundane trivialities, where we forget to look for him at all.

Warning: Wonder

By Ashlyn McKayla Ohm

I have no choice. I can't keep silent any longer. I have to share this caution with the world: *wonder is dangerous.*

Oh, I admit—wonder seems positive enough. No matter where or when or how we live, we've all welcomed—even pursued—its spark. We've felt its whisper-kiss in the first snowfall of winter or the brilliant blaze of the evening sky or the silk-rich shimmer of a hummingbird's wings. It's the ephemeral glow that seems to hover around the edges of existence, the unpredictable wind that blows against the hinges of the ordinary as we define it.

But despite this, I can't approach wonder with anything besides a warning. Because you see, wonder is as dangerous as poetry, or prayer, or love—all the volatile threats to a soul determined to stay asleep. (Souls, it turns out, are like kites—if they once get even a breath of wind beneath them, they'll be out of your hands and soaring to the skies before you can say *practicality*.)

Take it from one who knows. Even in childhood, I had all the risk factors for over-exposure to wonder. I was a homeschooled child, unattached to screens, deeply suspicious of popular opinion, and encouraged to ramble endlessly on our twenty-six acres of Arkansas countryside. That combination could not be more flammable, and wonder was ignited—both from the written world of science and math and literature, and from the witnessed world of silver streams and many-colored rocks and hawks that soared higher than Heaven itself.

Looking back on this perfect storm of subversion, it's not surprising that I became who I am today—a writer, a dreamer, a hiker, a wanderer of God's world who gets equally lost in the worlds inside my head and outside my window. In short, I'm eccentric—just as others gloomily predicted I would be—and the condition seems to be hopeless. At least, *hopeless* is the word written on their faces when they see me looking for birds with binoculars and a permanently uplifted face, murmuring plot ideas to myself while climbing the wooded ridges behind my home, or kneeling by the roadside to photograph a particularly delightful moss.

In other words, I've been incurably infected by wonder. I can't look away from this world—or forget that it is watching me in turn. I have lost my ability to go anonymous in life.

So be careful. If you live with your eyes open, this could happen to you too.

And if you would like to live a normal life—to blend into the monotone shadows around you, undisturbed by intrusive lightning-flashes from the transcendent—then you must avoid wonder, at all costs.

A clue as to why is found in the very origin of the word. It's a derivative of the Old English term *wundor*, meaning "marvelous thing, miracle, object of astonishment."[1] And therein lies the danger. When we marvel at this world of ours, we are tapping into something bigger than us—the miracle that undergirds all of existence. Furthermore, by noticing the miraculous, we are implicitly forced to question our safely sedate notions of reality. And sometimes, this questioning is inconvenient, threatening our schedules, our self-protection, our comforting assumptions about what is possible in this world.

But there's an even riskier component. You see, the equivalent German word for wonder, *wunder*, comes from a more ancient concept, a proto-Indo-European root that meant "to wish for, desire for, strive for."[2] More than just stoking our sense of the marvelous, wonder demands that we be honest about what we all "wish, desire, and strive for"—the raw and vulnerable pulse of our spirits that we seek to ignore or dismiss or downright suffocate. Wonder ignites the spark of eternity in our hearts,[3] tugging at the lodestone in each of us that stubbornly refuses to forget our spiritual home.

---

1 "Wonder," in Online Etymology Dictionary, https://www.etymonline. com/word/wonder#etymonline_v_10829.

2 "Wunder," in Wiktionary, last modified January 2, 2025, https://en.wiktionary.org/wiki/Wunder#:~:text=From%20Middle%20High%20German%20 wunder,%2C%20English%20wonder%2C%20Danish%20ounder.

3 Eccl 3:11.

This, then, is the fearsome power of wonder. It can not only startle our sleeping souls back to life but also radically reorder the world in which we awake. It cannot be received passively. It will not allow for the security of our human cognition or conceptions. In short, wonder throws open the door to capital-R Reality—not the narrow slice of the tangible, but the vast, unexplainable beyond. As a result, we are compelled to act, to change, to be transformed.

No surprise, then, that rather than embrace wonder, we often choose to anesthetize our spirits. In his excellent lecture "The Re-Enchanted World," writer and teacher Jonathan Rogers observes that as citizens of the modern world, we often close ourselves off to the beauty and glory that glimmer behind our stilted shadow version of reality.[4] His explanation for this is that we are frightened of the spiritual world beyond the limits of our control. And thus, rather than existing in what he calls a "porous" condition—allowing ourselves to soak up the spiritual—we snuggle into our layers of defense: cognitive habit and spiritual apathy and self-important distraction.

But despite our best efforts, wonder has a frustratingly relentless way of breaking through anyway. Songwriter John Mark McMillan sings of this in "Re-enchanted World": "I know that you've never been satisfied/With the numbers and the figures/But there's something still to find/...There's a Spirit in the night."[5] In CS Lewis's *The Screwtape Letters*, the demon Screwtape exasperatedly echoes this theme: "Even if we contrive to keep [humans] ignorant of explicit religion, the incalculable winds of fantasy and music and poetry—the mere face of a girl, the song of a bird, or the sight of a horizon—are always blowing our whole structure away."[6] Of course, this is the true power of wonder. Even the slightest moment of awe, the briefest glimpse of the transcendent, softens a part of our calloused souls. And as a result, we

---

4 Jonathan Rogers, "The Re-Enchanted World," October 11, 2024, Hutchmoot, Christ Community Church, Franklin, Tennessee, MP3, 01:27:35, https://store.rabbitroom.com/products/hutchmoot-2023-audio-archive-copy.

5 John Mark McMillan, "Re-Enchanted World," by John Mark McMillan, Lionhawk Records, track 8 on *Deep Magic*, 2023, Spotify app.

6 C. S. Lewis, *The Screwtape Letters* (New York: HarperOne, 1942), 156.

become, as Rogers would say, more porous beings—leaving our souls slightly less protected against the miraculous.

And in this, I think, wonder is like another radically risky thing: faith.

It's not surprising to me that one of Christ's own titles is *Wonderful.* Jesus Himself is the ultimate Wonder, the ultimate Reality, the ultimate Glory of which all other moments of awe are simply the dimmest of reflections. And he is not only the Creator but the Continuer—the One Who keeps wafting wonder through our world like a love song. Paul rejoices in this truth in Col. 1:16-17: "For by him all things were created, in heaven and on earth, visible and invisible, whether thrones or dominions or rulers or authorities—all things were created through him and for him. And he is before all things, and in him all things hold together" (ESV).

And what wonder demands from our attention, Christ compels from our hearts. When we enter into Him, we must be willing to become porous, to release our suppositions and suspicions, to discard all those beautiful biases and lovely lies. Fully, gloriously experiencing Him requires us to accept radical, unconditional vulnerability—laying ourselves bare to a Reality full of alarming (im)possibilities, to a Grace that is beautiful but terrible,[7] to a Love that is good beyond all goodness but is never, ever, safe.[8]

In the end, this is truly why wonder is so dangerous. Yes, it upends our preconceptions and cuts through our distractions and makes us tremble and weep and laugh again in the remembering of what we try to forget. But wonder's true power is that it is not a destination, but a path—a path that, if pursued to its ultimate end, will always lead us back to the Wonderful.

Perhaps this is part of the paradox Jesus offered His followers: "For whoever would save his life will lose it, but whoever loses his life for my sake will save it" (Luke 9:24 ESV). Wonder—like worship—is not forced upon us. We can choose to "save" our lives—keeping our heads down, our eyes closed, our ears covered. But

---

7 C. S. Lewis, *The Horse and His Boy* (New York: HarperCollins, 1954), 282.

8 C. S. Lewis, *The Lion, the Witch, and the Wardrobe* (New York: Harper-Collins, 1950), 146.

in the end, we will have simply yawned through life in a stupor, sidestepping pain, perhaps, but also purpose.

Or, we can lose our life—and thereby save it. We can come awake.

Today, right now, we can yield to the plea of McMillan's song: "So step away, step away, step away now from the white noise/ Bring your heart in, bring your heart in from the swirl/For the re-enchanted world."[9] We can open our eyes to sun-dazzled lakes and the bright brushstroke of a rainbow and the soaking silence of new snow. We can take a deep breath of freely given grace, all nerves tingling back to life, the relentless rush of Reality thrumming through our bones. And most of all, we can hold up our hesitant hearts to the Wonderful—allowing Him to show us the wonder not only in His breathtaking world, but in our own softening souls as well.

---

9 McMillan, "Re-Enchanted World."

The Incarnation and Play

By Sharon Rhyne

The velvet white head of a cat, stained by the kisses of a child whose lips are usually smeared with the evidence of lunch, rests on downy mountains of pink. If you picked her up, the pink mountains would come tumbling down, like the robes of a queen. A hair tie is secured below her ears, across the forehead, and a dried, brown Magnolia leaf sticks up in the center, as a feather. A white pearl necklace, plastic beads really, with a golden shell clasp rests royally on Kitty's neck.

Kitty is the beloved "child" of my eldest daughter. When she isn't being cuddled, kissed, and dramatically burped; she's her representative of all the emotions and thoughts a five-year-old finds hard to express.

"Kitty feels . . ." is the beginning of many Motherhood revelations for me, and I find that how Kitty views a scene is the most honest review. She frequently turns nine, which is the age of perfection, the time when five-year-olds believe they will finally be able to do all the hard things with ease.

"Kitty is nine today, and so she is sewing a new dress for her children," says a soft voice as I finish up dishes.

"Really? Do you want to learn to sew someday?"

"Maybe. When I'm nine."

Kitty is a lovey that the nursery magic[1] long ago turned into a real friend, and now she sits regal and stoic on the nursery floor, a Native princess, the prized audience of a freckled, blonde ballerina.

She sits between a lamb in a yellow frock covered in white daisies. The white piping around the collars is just starting to come away, a testament to the skill and diligence of my Mother's

---

1 Williams, Margery. 2004. *The Velveteen Rabbit*. London, England: Egmont Books.

sewing. The yellow frock is an old doll dress from when I was five and blonde and proud to be matching my dolls on an Easter Sunday morning, many Aprils ago. A series of finger puppet critters lean against a black and tanned striped mouse: the gift of Mr. Grey.

Mr. Grey surprised me one Tuesday morning with a trailer load of mulch for the garden I started building last Summer.

"Take a break, Sharon," he assured me as we unloaded, and I felt the corners of my eyes threatening black from exhaustion. Seeing stars at noon isn't a good sign. Unloading a trailer is the kind of hard work I, a suburban Mom, am not used to. But Mr. Grey is almost 80 years old, and my pride kept me huffing as we loaded fifty or more wheelbarrows, scattering them about the paths.

"How does he do it?" my husband and I exclaimed, as he drove away and we collapsed on the couch.

My daughter had a fever that morning, and she sat at the window watching us work. The next morning, before I could catch my breath, Mr. Grey knocked again; this time with a trailer load of manure and a mouse to comfort the girl with the fever.

It's lumpy and rough, as if its fur has been soaked in tears many times. My five-year-old was not the first child to love this mouse, though she instantly saw its value. Mouse, for that was its name, was clearly real to her, a real friend, a real comfort. But she did not make him real. Some other child, maybe a son now grown-up but still prayed for, had loved this mouse into a state of honor. She simply recognized all the signs and immediately moved Mouse to a place of authority in the nursery. Real toys command respect, and she knew, as I know the look in the eyes of a woman who has buried a child, that Mouse had once deeply mattered to some child, much as Mr. Grey did.

The finger puppets, Kitty, Mouse, me, and a host of rabbits, elephants, dogs, bears, and Polly Pockets sit expectantly in a circle, an imaginary canopy overhead. The circus has come to town, and this afternoon we are playing "opening night."

Playing with my daughter didn't come naturally to me, still doesn't. I find myself embarrassed to admit that many times I have to write "play" in my list of things to do. If I don't, I usually won't do it. I don't like to play.

It's not that I don't enjoy spending time with her. We make bread, take walks, read armfuls of books, work, and wander. We spend all day together delighting and debating and pretending. It's a joy to me, and yet, play is the one time I find myself forced. It's as unnatural to me as it is natural to her.

"Why is that?" I wonder, as I sit on her bedroom floor, pretending to rock a crying buffalo to sleep. This act of pretending with her on her terms in her realm is the greatest sign of love I can give her. She tells me so in a thousand ways, the most poignant being when I made my New Year Resolutions:

"What do you think? What do YOU want to do more of this year, darling?"

She thinks silent, stoic, her smooth round face the most beautiful I have ever seen, before she cuts through the world of adulthood with sharp innocence:

"Play more with Mommy."

And I know that I must make play important in 2025.

This is my Motherhood faithfulness, but it may not be yours. My daughter is my only living child. She does not have playmates in the way I did, where an afternoon outside with my many siblings was a delight. She is frequently lonely. This is a trial I did not see coming in her life, for I am one of nine. I was never alone, and therefore, my imagination for what Motherhood would look like desperately needs expanding. Over the last five years, I have discovered that I must stop, in small ways, trying to be like my Mother and more like the Mother of my daughter. This means I must learn to play.

I think over the many Mr. Greys of my life. Elderly friends; selfless aunts; neighbors, Sunday school teachers; Grandpa–what in them did I admire most? It was their ability to fall joyously onto a living room floor with stuffies and legos; to imagine worlds within a child's world, to build sand castles with toddlers. This ability to deeply enjoy the life of play seems to be the mark of sainthood, and so I wonder at the beauty I do not yet enjoy. Why? Why don't I?

It is the thoughts I struggle with that I am most interested in, the dangerous thoughts where my own defects could surface. I, like Kitty, long to be real, as real as love allows. I want to be real in the eyes of my Creator and real in the life of my daughter, not just some ancient legend at the edges of her vision. I know this includes losing hair and being stained. I must look more like Mr. Grey, show up not with what I would give, but what is needed. I must submit myself to the wonders of the nursery magic, the painful work of becoming, the dragon skin peeling away as it once did for Eustace[2]; and so I explore that question.

"Why do I struggle to play?"

Maybe it is because I have not understood the tangible, physical, playful nature of my God. Or if I have understood it, I've kept it locked away in the kitchen of Christianity, believing he is busy doing real work. And yet, if Christmas is to seep into the cracks of the year, if light really has shown in the midst of darkness, then surely it was beautiful and real and just what our world needed? And if Christ came to my world as one of us, can't I come to hers?

I write this on the second Sunday of Epiphany, when the church remembers the miracle of Cana. I rarely think about the miracle of water becoming wine because it seems like such a small one, insignificant. I tend to rate the miracles of scripture by accomplishment and ability, healing and relief. I rate his miracles by human standards because I am a woman who struggles to play. He sees the pinnacle of human play, a wedding feast, and enhances the moment. He provided for their play in the flow of beauty and joy, red and rich and sweet; the best wine for last because men were designed to laugh.

I can hear their laughter, feel the relief of a hostess caught in an awkward dilemma. I can taste the delight of guests discovering that just a little longer, they would be allowed to feast. The five more minutes plea of a child whose greatest goal in life is to play with Mommy. The joy of men who's greatest joy is to know and enjoy God forever, and how can that be if He will not come to us? How can that be, if I will not join her?

---

2 C. S. Lewis, *The Voyage of the Dawn Treader*, (New York, HarperCollins Publishers, 1980) pg. 109

Maybe that's it. Maybe I am too consumed with working for my Father than with enjoying his gifts. When did I last delight in the "sunshine of his face?"[3]

We load our stuffies, Lamb and Kitty and Mouse, into a pink stroller. I have placed a purple rabbit, the largest of her "children" into the stroller she once rode around in, and off we go, into the sunshine of a late afternoon. It is a warm day, a short reprieve before our next freeze, and the birds dot the power lines, bellies turned to the sun. We are Mother rabbits taking our children for a stroll. I do the best rabbit voice I can, but I am not just a Mother playing with her child.

I am a child too, playing with the gifts of my Father, turning to feel the real sun on my real skin. I have come to her world because he came to mine, and in coming, I find the wonders around me have brought me back to him. Maybe this play is a small part of becoming like Christ.

Here on a quiet afternoon of imagination, I see glory in the insignificance of pretending; the joy of becoming, and in coming I am building the language of the soul that one day, when she forgets how to play, maybe I can whisper the wonder of the nursery magic.

"You are real, daughter; made to be real. Come, let us play first as Mother and daughter; soon as saints."

---

3 Elizabeth C. D. Clephane, "Beneath the Cross of Jesus,"

The Pebbles Moms Carry

By April Ficklin

On the day I brought my tiny blonde darling home from the hospital, I rocked her to the whispered creak of a white wooden chair and cried.

Time had stood still during her delivery just a few days prior as my obstetrician had lovingly turned my baby girl's face to me. Seconds before she was fully born, I had the first look into her grey-blue eyes. This was awe.

Her tiny pink nose, the wisps of hair touching the back of her neck, the way she melted into the cradle of my arms after whimpering for me—these were the joys of new motherhood. I had been anxious about her birth as I treasured her safety in my womb for months and knew that the moment she was born, new fears would creep in. But, in those first few moments and days, we found a vulnerable and powerful bond. Everything wasn't easy or magical in the beginning; in fact, nursing my new baby was one of the biggest challenges of my life, and I wasn't exactly suited for sleep deprivation, but the strength of our connection was instant. This was awe.

But I silently cried in that chair on that first day home because, just as wonderstruck as I was sitting in the pink and brown nursery I had carefully curated for my firstborn, I was also suddenly overcome with sorrow. I instantly understood just how quickly this sweet baby, this loyal attachment, this new role of mine, this fresh delight was going to change. This was grief.

I recognized that though her life was just getting started, I'd never have as much time to watch her fall asleep in my arms, to twist her curls in my hands, to feel her fingers squeeze mine as I'd like. And I was right. Too quickly, her baby smirks would turn into toddler giggles, and her living room dances would turn into waltzes into the kindergarten classroom. Every new marvelous season would fade into the next without warning. This was grief.

Days into my motherhood journey, I learned that I'd spend the rest of my life carrying them both: awe and grief. Like small pebbles slipped into a pocket and jostled around each time my hands found them again, I'd re-discover these dichotomous feelings over and over throughout her childhood.

In kindergarten, she held my hand on a school bus full of chatter as we turned into the zoo parking lot. In fourth grade, she asked me not to chaperone the trip to Atlanta. When she was in elementary school, I'd tuck her into bed and read *Sarah Plain and Tall* or *Charlie and the Chocolate Factory*, and she'd give me extra hugs after to keep me in her room just a little bit longer. By the end of middle school, she was drifting off to sleep with her book light still on and the newest young adult novel by her side. During her junior year, she sat on a hard bench next to me at the Globe Theater in London, marveling at Othello. Just months later, she was filling out college applications. Every moment I got to hold her close was coupled with another in which I'd have to let her go just a little bit more.

That's the journey. And what I've learned from it is that both the awe and grief are transformative. Of course, my daughter has been transforming into an incredibly amazing adult over the last eighteen years, but that's not the only reworking. These years of motherhood have been an undoing and rebuilding, a reckoning and regrowing, a breaking and healing for me. I've rewritten so many aspects of who I am while figuring out what being a mother should be: success is now defined by connection rather than achievement, wealth is measured in rich moments instead of dollars, and the need for acknowledgement gave way to the desire for deep conversation.

I'm sure I'll continue to grieve the brevity of our time together as she takes steps into her future, but I'm also sure I will never stop living in awe of being her mom. As she's gotten older, she's asked a few times, "When do we get to be friends?" This question comes because I've always explained that right now I have to focus on being a good mother to her, but one day, when she reaches adulthood, we will definitely be friends, too. And now I can let her know we are almost there.

Live the Wonder

By Aly Prades

My alarm breaks the silence of the inky dark and I force myself to roll out of bed. Before I check my phone, before I search the covers for my glasses, or sneak into the bathroom without waking my husband, I pad my way over to the window and draw back the curtain.

The red and white Christmas lights illuminate the front porch with just enough glow to answer my question.

Snow?

***

I swirl the colors on my watercolor palette and watch as they blend. *Paint like a child*, I think of Julia Cameron saying. *Embrace a childlike wonder, a glee and freedom you felt before the world told you art and life had to look a certain way.*

I think of myself as a child, how painting usually ended in tears. How I made my mom draw the pictures for my book reports. How I enlisted a senior boy to sketch my poster for the Mothers Against Drunk Driving poster contest. How I won 3rd place in that contest and accepted the award while gulping down guilt.

Childlike wonder?

I think of my own children and their balled up and crossed out art projects. I see it in them too: the frustration that reality never lives up to the picture in their head. I keep swirling the colors on my palette. Dab tiny strokes across the page.

Can I really let go?

***

I plan my exit strategy to a T. Bikini for easy removal. Two towels held up by my dad and husband so I can strip off the icy swimsuit. A quick towel dry and shuffle into a dry fleece shirt and snow pants. Shake the sand from my toes, then socks, rain boots. Parka over all of it for the walk back to the car.

I did not plan what to do when I hit the water. Tiny snowflakes flutter by almost imperceptibly. Blink and you'll miss them. Lake water in the low 40s. Pine trees dusted with snow.

I give a quick wave to my family and hear the countdown.

No time to think or second-guess.

Three...two...one!

The whistle sounds and I shuffle and almost stumble as I dive in.

I don't register cold, just shock, transition. I had wanted to stay in longer, but the participants around me are already running back to shore.

I stand up and my hands burn, the air feels scalding, not cold.

But my breath doesn't catch. I'm awake and alive.

I did the thing! I moved toward the discomfort on purpose! Quite literally plunged in and came out the other side.

Do I have the resolve to stay?

***

When I think about the wonder of a child, I wonder what happened to me. I remember building my blocks in numerical order and ripping up book reports because my drawings didn't match the cover. I remember sending myself to my room and crying over missed spelling words. There was lots of love in my house, snuggles with Mom, Dad singing the Star-Spangled Banner and Take Me Out to the Ball Game before bed, siblings to fight and play Ninja Turtles with, but my mind gave way to dark wonders and what ifs more often than delight and glee. I spent more time battling the questions in my head than living the life in front of me.

Wonder for me as a child looked like: I wonder if those fireworks will come down and burn me, I wonder why my drawing never matches the picture, I wonder if my grandmother is going to hell, I wonder if my heart was pure when I said the sinner's prayer, I wonder if I should let Jesus into my heart again, just in case, I wonder if my stuffed animals hate me because I didn't rotate them, I wonder if Mrs. Rossi knows my mom helped with my book report, I wonder if God knows I snuck a taste of my brownie before I finished my broccoli, I wonder if Ms. Wallace knows I looked at Kayla L.'s paper for that times-table answer, I wonder if Mom knows I tricked Cameron, my little brother, into touching the electric fence, again, I wonder if everyone knows, I'm bad bad bad.

I was diagnosed with Obsessive-Compulsive Disorder when I was 35-years-old. The diagnosis explained so much of my childhood experience with looping fears that I wasn't good enough. Finally getting access to appropriate tools and therapy has helped quiet the recurrent fears. After spending years trying to will away my worry or try harder to be a more grateful Christian, it was OCD therapy that helped me actually learn to live out—and believe—God's love for me. Through my diagnosis and recovery, God has held me. Healing my mental health has really just been a return to knowing who I've been all along: loved by God.

I was so relieved when I was diagnosed with OCD that it never occurred to me to be sad that I had OCD in the first place. I'm starting to feel sad for that little girl. Some days I question why worry and fear, rules and shoulds, stole moments of joy from my childhood. Since being diagnosed with OCD, I've used my words and writing to bring awareness to this often misunderstood condition. Some days I want to quit writing about OCD altogether. OCD stole so much already, will it steal my writing, too? Do I have anything else to write about? What's real Aly and what's just the me made in defense of OCD? Can they be disentangled?

Alongside the questions and the sadness, gratitude springs up. Not cheap, toxic positivity, but a real awe that I am not where I once was. My brain is enticed by curiosity and delight, where it was once driven by fear. My wonders these days sound more like the wonders of a child without OCD.

Wonder today sounds like: I wonder what life would be like in a new city, I wonder what a cold plunge would feel like, I wonder if I can write a memoir, I wonder if I'll like my first Idaho winter, I wonder where the day will take me, I wonder if my kids would like rock climbing, tap dance, cooking class, I wonder what a day without my phone would feel like, I wonder if I'd enjoy rock climbing, tap dance, cooking class, I wonder if I'd like to watercolor, I wonder what would feel good to do today.

To be alive is to accept the good and the hard and the annoying paradox that you often can't have the good without the hard.

I'm learning to let the sadness and the gratitude wash over me like a dusting of snowflakes, like swirling watercolors, like a sharp plunge into a frigid lake. I'm learning to leave the questions unanswered in my head and live the wonder instead.

A Simple Breath Prayer

By Kathy Young

I hear crying. It's 6 a.m. I pull the blanket over my head, let it swallow me whole, and pretend not to hear my one-year-old daughter weeping from the nursery. But there's no ignoring the piercing sound of her cries. She's up, which means I am too.

I slip on a pair of leggings and my favorite hoodie—the one that says "HOMEBODY" in all caps across the front. These days, it seems like a fitting title. And yes, it's the same outfit I wore yesterday, but I let it slide.

My mind is groggy as I step into her room. Normally, my daughter wouldn't be awake this early, but with the fever she's been battling, early mornings have become the new normal. She looks up at me with puffy eyes, tears streaming down her face. I scoop her up from the crib and let the warmth of her little body press against mine. I could spend this moment brooding over the fact that I've lost my precious morning "me time," but I don't. Instead, I inhale, exhale, and pull her in close. We stand there in the dark, huddled together, and a tender joy ripples in my heart as I embrace her. I wonder if, by now, she knows that Mommy is a safe space. I hope she does. *She won't always need you like this*, I remind myself. *For now, just be right here.*

In between sobs, I continue to kiss her head of tangled curls until eventually, she's calm. Then we make the journey downstairs. I've mastered this routine already; I've been through it before. And I know by now that this will be the start of a long day.

I settle onto the couch, hoping to rest my eyes while she drinks her bottle. But before I know it, I'm drifting in and out of sleep. It's not long before I feel her small hand gently tap my shoulder, which startles me awake. It's 7 a.m. now. Only 7 a.m. and I'm exhausted. How am I supposed to make it through the rest of the day like this?

I wish it weren't always this way—I really do—but more often than not, it takes being cornered in my weakness for me to realize how much I need a fresh encounter with the Lord. With a sigh, I flip open my Bible and turn to 1 Chronicles. I've been working my way through genealogies, and I'll be honest, it's not exactly a page-turner. But as I keep reading, between the endless lists of names, a verse about the Reubenites prompts me to pause:

"For they cried out to God in the battle, and he granted their urgent plea because they trusted in Him" (1 Chron. 5:20 ESV).

I pause and quietly reflect: *Do I trust God to fight my battles? Am I bringing my urgent pleas to him? If I truly believed he is Lord of all, wouldn't I trust him to sustain me through this day?*

While my daughter plays with her mega blocks on the floor, I whisper a simple breath prayer:

Lord, give me the energy to play with my daughter.

It's not like I was suddenly hit with a burst of Holy Spirit energy while sitting there on the living room floor. No, nothing like that. It was more like I was given a quiet understanding. A quiet understanding that although I am sleep-deprived, the Lord will provide the daily bread that I need to play with my daughter, just for today, just for this moment. And sure enough, He did. I felt Him in every board book we flipped, every silly face we made, and every game of chase we played over the next several hours. It was as if the more I exerted myself with my daughter, the more I felt the Lord's spirit of rest wash over me. Then, I glance at the clock to realize that praise God I've made it—it's finally time for her afternoon nap.

On a day like this, I'd usually want to nap too, but today is different. Today, come to think of it, I do feel a bit more energized. In fact, I think today I have it in me to surprise my husband with a clean house before he gets home from work—a rare occurrence in the Young household. So, I tie up my hair and get to work. I wash the dishes spilled over the kitchen sink, put away laundry left over from the weekend, and pick up the toys in the playroom. Only after all that do I feel a deep sense of satisfaction. Now, I can finally rest—and I do.

As the day winds down, I hear the familiar sound of my husband's car pulling into the driveway. It's the signal for our little "Daddy's home!" celebration. The door swings open, and there he is, grinning wide. "How was your day?" he asks, his voice warm as he steps into the kitchen. I smile, knowing that despite the exhaustion, the day has been a good one. I share with him what I had read in 1 Chronicles and how I felt a sense of renewal today.

Then I turn the question back to him. "How was your day—what was your favorite part?" He pauses, his gaze softening as he looks at me. "Honestly," he says, "Right now. Knowing you had a special day with our girl and felt the joy of the Lord."

Truth be told, most days, I struggle to feel the joy of the Lord. Nurturing a home and raising my child is a quiet labor. Efforts often go unseen and unnoticed; and yet, it's what fills me with glorious purpose. This afternoon, the Lord met me, in our home, in our midst. He fueled me to do good, honest work with my hands and be present with my daughter. I take this moment to acknowledge that the King of the Universe granted my urgent plea. I only pray that I continue to see glimmers of his glory right before my very eyes.

A Day of Small Things

By Charis Crandall

The night rain turned to day rain without missing a drop. I stood at the trailhead in drizzle and fog, surrounded by impressive glacier-topped peaks I could not see. Sodden clouds shrouded the expansive vistas I longed for, but I *needed* to hike this trail on this day. Spurred on by a wild hope that the mountains would eventually shoulder the clouds off to the side, I adjusted the hood on my rain jacket, shrugged into my backpack, and gathered my determination.

The lower section of trail followed a river, which on a sunny day would have tumbled happily down its course to a larger river in the valley below. Today, the rain enraged it, transformed it into a bellowing tumult that rose up out of the fog to crash over boulders and thrash against its banks. Only gravity could affect any restraint on its angry surge. Here was majesty and force as awe-inspiring as any wind-buffeted summit.

Resigned to cloud-restricted views, I ducked my head into the rain and watched the trail reveal itself one step at a time. Steps accumulated into miles, and each mile revealed wonders I would not likely have noticed if my eyes had been drawn upward to the peaks I knew stood guard on every side. I watched silvery rivulets wander over the trail and braid themselves into adventurous streams. Thimbleberry leaves palmed single raindrops, cradled them until enough drops collected to cause a leaf-tip and a drip-fall. Trail rocks cleansed of monochromatic dust glistened green, rust, red, white, black. Trees gripped fistfuls of mountainside to anchor themselves against wind and gravity, their twisted roots providing shelter for miniature forests of fungi. Brilliant orange and pale green lichens freckled trailside granite boulders. Wood lilies and mountain arnica hooded their faces from the rain but failed to hide their colors, echoes of sunshine nestled in variegated green foliage.

A series of waterfalls divide the steep upper trail into convenient distance markers. I could hear its thunder long before the first waterfall appeared like a phantom out of the fog, perpetually pouring out of nowhere into nothingness far below. Another one, swollen far beyond its usual boundaries, left me with the impression that the mountain was crying, its tears gushing from barely visible cracks and fissures.

Above the waterfalls, a long, lonely stretch of barren scree felt even longer and more isolated in the dense smurr. With nothing to look at here but shards of shale beneath my feet, my sight turned inward to an image of my oldest son traversing this same scree slope several years before. I could hear his words whisper-yelled into my ear over the roar of the last waterfall: "God is an amazing landscape designer, isn't he?" *Yes, he is, my son. I lament that you ultimately failed to understand how he also designed you—for a purpose, for life.* If there was any point on the trail where I needed the glory of snow-crowned mountains against a cerulean blue sky, this was it. Wouldn't that wondrous, awe-inspiring view renew my vision of the Most High God, Master Designer of Landscapes and Life? The opaque, veiled world around me felt too much like the grief I was trying to climb over and around and above.

After the scree came an equally barren rock-strewn 'moonscape,' evidence that a glacier once crept here. One final stream marked the edge of this ancient glacier trail, and like every other stream, river, and waterfall, it had gorged itself on the continuous rain. A heavy plank served as a sturdy foot-bridge, but the stream-turned-torrent mocked such a contraption, boiling over it with abandon. I felt the vibrations as soon as I stepped onto the wooden board; the enraged waters picked up and propelled glacier-worn rocks, tumbled them against the bridge, and sent a palpable beat into my entire body. *Thump-thump, thump-thump.* The heartbeat of a mountain. The heartbeat of God for people like me swollen with grief, tumbling from what was into the question mark of what is and what will be, spilling beyond boundaries that once felt as solid as the mountains so present yet invisible around me.

I hiked that day because I sought the exhilaration of standing before the grandiose and majestic. Even more, I needed to sense that God was *more* majestic, *more* exalted than his created world, and certainly more than the mountainous ache in my heart. Instead, what I encountered in the endless drizzle and grey was an immanent God of small things. He was as present in the stubby alpine anemones and sprawling lichens as in the mountains I thought I desperately needed to see. He was as near as the relentless rain and cataclysmic rivers that saturated my clothes and sloshed in my boots. He was wholly above and beyond my grief and fully present in every moment of it. He was who he declared himself to be in Christ: *Emmanuel,* God with us—a not-small thing on any day.

Hidden

By Mary Madeline Schumpert

I keep noticing You hidden. Tucked into the conversation I had with a friend about all the woes and worries of this temporary home. I keep seeing You twinkling through the song on my Spotify. I keep hearing You, somehow, wordlessly whisper to me in the afternoon wind. I keep wondering if my desire to scream out this Good News—despite the social repercussions—is Your divine pushing. Are You grinning right now, because I'm finally noticing? I saw a flicker of Your kindness in my soul as I was on my knees this morning. Endorphins maybe? No. No, no. Something holier. Other-worldly.

I want to be convinced it is all coincidence. It feels safer there, in delusion. I want to say that it's not You. This makes me seem smarter, more wise, less naïve, less optimistic, more accepted. Safe from cynical stares, from laughter. I am tempted to cover all of my highest, most sacred belief in skepticism, but today I don't. I will stand mocked by my own old self, and those who can't see. I'm finally learning how to cope without acceptance of either.

You see, I can't do without Your intricate details much anymore, and logical or not (depending on the source), I'm beginning to think chance is only truth by the promise of Your providence, stretching into the tiniest little details, sprinkled throughout our most mundane moments. It's always expanding into the tiniest and biggest moments. There is no place this Good News doesn't touch.

I wonder if, up to now, I've spent my whole second life drowning in my first birth. And You have been trying to hold my hand, pull me up, let my toes find a way above the waves, let my feet glide and spin on the seeming chaos of it all.

And I am Peter, with faith half the size of a mustard seed, once walking, now drowning.

But I want to dance.
Won't You grow it? Please?
Ah, yes— that's just it:
You are.
I think I'm finally listening, with ears to hear.
Finally seeing, with eyes to see.

Springtime of the Soul

How much delight can You squeeze out of me?

No—*seriously*. I cannot number the giggles that are rising, bubbling in my cup, tipping over. I am on my daily walk, this time, dancing with the trees, the Wind whipping through the souls of us both. *Look out the window—there's a grown twenty-six-year-old, spinning on the sidewalk.*

Whole-bodied laughter and wind gusts of glee, true joy masked as *ditsy*. I have retraced my steps to and from this same old tree stump every day for the past six months, and yet You have numbered each one different, set it apart, distinct. Holy. A new joy You let loose, to run and roam in my home of heart. I am an eager, gracious host.

I'm trying to catch every laugh and pocket it safe, save it for another day when I can't seem to remember the outline of Your face. You must have fun watching this scene unfold, thunder of laughter vibrating from the Throne Room.

The axis of this universe is tipping toward grace—happily!—always, forever—constantly. This fact dissolves me dizzy with delight.

And do tell—*how much delight have I wrung out of You?*

With Your tip-tip-tipping, always, every morning, new. With Your boundless hope seeping out of the earth and into my toes, saturating my bloodstream, covering every inch of me, reaching higher, higher, *higher are Your thoughts*—reaching, stretching into the atmosphere and raining down, all over again.

I'm jumping up and down again, trying to gather them all and snuggle them close, squeeze out all Your goodness and gulp it down. The Trinity is like a water-cycle mystery: grace can be recycled and never worn out. Yet You provide new ones: more, more, more, each moment, washing over me.

How much delight pours down from the heavens and wisps through the trees, as I breathe it in— oh Good One in Three? Oh goodness, Goodness, God-ness raining down on me.

This is what it means that the joy of the Lord is armor. Strength is clothed in the humility of delight.

I am free—so very free from the old slavery of me.

I am rich! Yes, oh very rich indeed.

Grace is the sun; mercy, the air I breathe.

And whole-hearted love?—

it's without number, free,

the ground beneath my very feet.

Rediscovering the Wonder of Winter

By Christy Lynne Wood

I stood at the top of the hill, my heart pounding, as I gulped breaths of icy air. My cheeks felt hot and cold, and a trickle of sweat made its way down my chest. As my heartbeat slowed, I focused on noticing every sensation in my body. The snow-covered forest around me stood silent and still. I was alone, and I've never felt more alive. I swung my poles forward and continued my snowshoed tromp downward. Marked with small green circles, the trail I followed curved through the trees—unbroken except for deer prints crisscrossing it here and there. The temperature hovered at ten degrees without considering windchill, but it didn't matter. This new winter sport had hooked me, and I would be back out again soon.

The first time I put on snowshoes and tried to stand up, I fell over like a toddler on my hands and knees. The second time was better, and I slowly got the hang of moving. It helped that I found poles which made balancing and staying upright much easier. Snowshoeing took effort, but there was a beauty and freedom to it that I didn't expect. My adventures shocked me, mostly because I enjoyed being outdoors in winter again. Perhaps God had answered my prayers.

I don't remember when I started struggling with winter as an adult, but each year it seemed to get worse. Christmas snow in December made me happy. I tolerated the cold in January, but by February my tolerance evaporated and left me irritated and grumpy. Unfortunately for me, I live in Michigan where we have winterish weather for five to six months of the year. The cold bothered me, but the abject lack of sunshine left me depressed. Michigan winters are mostly gray and overcast, and they seem to last forever—well into months that should be spring.

As a child, I loved winter. I built forts, went cross-country skiing, enjoyed sledding, and dug tunnels in snow drifts. I happily curled up with a pile of books, drank hot chocolate, and snuggled down under a mound of blankets at night. But somehow, I lost the wonder as an adult. And the more I hated winter, the longer it seemed to last. I was miserable, but I did not want to waste my time hating half of each year. So, I began to pray, and I also began to look for joy in this season of cold, snow, and darkness.

The Norwegian concept of *hygge* intrigued me and I began to focus on all things cozy and comfortable in the winter. Over the next few years, I bought a ridiculous number of fuzzy blankets, made sure to light candles, and drank gallons of hot tea. When I went outside, I bundled up and intentionally breathed the cold air. I felt the shiver in my lungs and the tingle on my face. As someone who regularly swims in Lake Superior each summer, I enjoy a good frigid plunge. The winter air felt familiar in its intensity and energy.

Last winter I noticed a definite difference. We had a couple of big snowstorms and both times I dressed warmly and went down to the river behind our house to explore. It felt like I was wandering around Narnia. I came back home feeling refreshed and amazed. Our snow only lasted a couple of weeks last year and I wondered if my improved attitude came from the shortness of the season or if I had truly changed. Either way, I survived winter more successfully than I have in years.

I changed jobs this year and went from working as a fifth-grade math teacher to being a behavior support specialist. Part of my new job includes three periods outside each day: drop-off, pick-up, and recess duty. I spend over an hour and a half outside in all kinds of weather. During the winter, my snowpants come on and off three times each day. Strangely enough, I don't mind.

In the deep winter, darkness was just fading when I went out in the mornings. The snowflakes falling in the beams from the parking lot light poles were magical. I gazed upwards and smiled to myself. Running the sledding hill for kindergarteners and then first and second graders was a little nerve-wracking and a whole lot of fun. I watch them be brave, scream, giggle, tumble off into the snow, and come gasping back for more. I caught every elusive sunbeam that came out in the afternoon. I'd lift my face, close my eyes, and bask in them. Winter has somehow seemed shorter and more beautiful this year.

My snowshoeing adventures happened on a solo trip to a tiny cabin in the woods. It snowed constantly and the air temperature was ten degrees or less all weekend. But I bundled up and adventured out three times. Each time I came home with a smile on my face and peace in my heart. I've taken my children cross-country and downhill skiing this year. I've dragged my husband on snowy tromps down by our river. One night I took a walk in our neighborhood in the middle of a snowstorm just because I wanted to. The wind and snow stung my face, and I laughed. My childlike wonder has returned.

Fuzzy blankets, candles, and gallons of tea are still my friends during this cold and gray time of the year. But I have also discovered a new beauty and delight in the crisp, invigorating air, the sparkling snowflakes, and even the gray clouds that make one sunbeam feel like a gift. I know that much of this change in my attitude is a direct answer to prayer, but I think it's also due to the way I've chosen to accept and dive into enjoying winter.

It's almost March. There's a small part of me that is sad to see the snow leave. I'll miss the way the arctic air kisses my cheeks and burns my lungs. But I'm also enjoying watching the seasons change. At recess I can hear the melting snow trickling down the drain pipes from the roof. The birds are singing, and the sun on my skin feels warmer every day. I'm not in a hurry for spring this year. We will probably get at least one more snowstorm; after all, I do live in Michigan. And when it comes, I'll enjoy it even more because I know it won't last.

The cycles that God built into our world are comforting to me. Seasons come, go, and come again. Snow falls and melts. The light slowly disappears as each day gets darker until one day the light begins to reappear again. I feel the rhythms, the predictable changes, and I find hope. There is beauty in the changing seasons—each one so different from the others. Change is good for us even though it can be uncomfortable. The change in my heart as God has worked these past few years is very good. I feel satisfying peace, unexpected joy, and renewed wonder as I rest in the coziness of these last few days of winter.

When Wild Hearts Dance

By Kelly Meagher

I took him out to the woods. Each of us, a muffin in hand, snacking on breakfast as we made our way through the soft morning fog. Suspensions on the third day of kindergarten don't bode well for little souls trying to make their way in the world. So, I took his wild little heart out into the wilderness where maybe it would feel at home—grounded. They say nature vibrates at the same frequency of love, and what better way to recoup than having all of creation sing out, "I love you".

We scouted out the marked trees directing our way to the river, picking up fallen acorns along the way. He filled his pockets, and we talked about what the acorns would have become had he left them. Some become food, some give themselves back to the soil, and a few find the right place to grow and become mighty oaks. I realized as we talked that the forest not only teaches us how to be loved, but how to live. How to be and die and resurrect and start again, and that no solitary moment is the whole of things. And I breathed a sigh of relief—a sigh of hope that this little soul walking alongside me would indeed make it. Kindergarten, after all, never makes it onto transcripts or resumes.

In all their faithfulness, the painted oaks carried us to the river. He immediately asked for the uncharted path: downhill, full of overgrowth and fallen trees, with a sure bet a bed of mud would be lying underneath. His Crocs alone weren't going to survive that trip.

"How about we find another way?"

And we did.

We followed the path further than either of us had ever gone and landed on the sandy banks of the small brook. He took out his handful of acorns and started tossing them in the water. A cathartic act. I tried skipping a few rocks to his immediate protest. Convinced his acorns were better for the environment than my rocks, he insisted I stop. Acorns float down river and disintegrate after all, whereas rocks sink to the bottom and stay forever. So, we threw acorns—he caring for the environment as I puzzled out how to care for his soul.

Should I bring up school?

Not yet.

I waited and pried as we walked back through the muddy trails of the forest. He threw up an imaginative tale as to why he wasn't in school that day, and not wanting to betray his mother's words, I let it go. He certainly didn't lack intelligence or wit, and I marveled at his imagination. Still, I skirted the defensive play and started talking about vases and how they are made to hold pretty flowers. Maybe we could go pick out a few? His little boy mind only heard "bases" and he asked if maybe we could just build one here in the woods. No attempt to clarify the word worked, so we finished our morning walking dreaming up what kind of fort we would build and how long we should stay. Together we decided our beds were a must have and he thought maybe a refrigerator too. We'd stay a few days and go home for the weekend. It was a convenient plan for a conflicted soul.

An hour spent in the wilderness, and we headed out to a much more tamed world. Out where manicured lawns sat surrounded by blocks of pavement and the trees were told where they could grow. As we drove past rows of uniform houses canopied with webs of electrical lines, I wondered at which frequency the pavement vibrated. Certainly, it wasn't love.

We pulled into the parking lot and headed into the store. The LED lights overhead and plastic merchandise resting on cold metal shelves felt like a stark contrast to our morning venture. And yet this is the substance we've made our lives of—trading the order of creation for our man-made chaos. To live under buzzing lights and white walls instead of the wonder of what nature has to teach us. His soul rebels against it and we frown at his rebellion, and yet, how desperately I try to daily pull my own soul away from the lull of man-made things.

Because even this morning, amidst deadlines and unfinished projects and the rhythm and agendas of daily life, I barely held my own soul at bay to bend to the beautiful wilderness of a little boy's heart that needed tending. I, myself, had almost missed the invitation. The invitation to break from the man-made demands and expectations and rediscover the wonder and beauty God has placed in all that he has made.

We made our way to the manufactured vases, and I bent down to once again explain what they were for and asked him who we might give them to? Maybe a teacher or two? I set a variety on the lower shelf so he could choose, and we walked to the front, vases in hand, where he handed the cashier a bill. We talked about what flowers we would pick to go inside. He thought plastic flowers would be nice—the kind that sat in the green bin near the check-out counter. And I thought maybe something a little more real—something a little more untame; something that vibrated at the frequency of love.

He settled on a bouquet of pink mini roses along with a grouping of wild flowers, and I thought them to be perfectly balanced. I whispered a prayer that his teachers might too recognize the beauty of the mixture of domesticated and wild things. Because as civilized as we all try to be, we were created from and for a much more untamed world, and God continues to plant among us these wild little hearts who refuse to forget the beat to which we were made to dance. Like the trees, we try to tame and control them, "Grow here. Don't spill over your allotted space there." But, when we take the time to bow and see what this ruckus is all about, we find ourselves taken to the wilderness, being reminded that we are loved, and tuning our hearts to the frequency in which we were made to live.

A Royal Invitation

By Awara Fernández

"Come into my castle and have lunch with me."

This invitation was issued to me by my granddaughter, Anna, during a trip to a local children's museum, a magical space that is a favorite of my grandchildren. That day, I was there with my daughter, Amanda, along with 5 Littles all under the age of 8. Since there were at least another 899 Littles with their assorted caregivers hurtling around the room, I spent our time there moving back and forth between the various playscapes while counting heads:

"One, two, three, four, five. All safe. One, two, three, four . . . where's five? Ah, okay. All safe. One . . . where's two?"

And there she was, Princess Anna of the Castle (number two accounted for), leaning over the rampart, blonde hair flowing over her shoulders, royal gown bunched up around her neck, pink glasses askew. I was already moving on to look for number three when I heard her voice call out to me, "Nana, come into my castle and have lunch with me." Because we know the voices of the people we love, I heard her clearly over the din of 899 other treble voices raised in delighted squeals.

And, I almost walked on by, forfeiting the chance to have lunch with a princess, because duty was calling. I almost missed it. But, as I paused and looked at her face, beaming with joy, I remembered that Amanda was also watching over the children, keeping track of them. And, the only way out of the museum was through a Gate with a Gate-Keeper intoning, "None Shall Pass," unless accompanied by a parent or caregiver. I could stop counting heads for a moment.

So, I ducked under the doorway in the castle wall and was greeted by a tiny princess who ushered me into her tiny kingdom. Taking her hostessing duties seriously, she brought me a tiny plate filled with her best plastic food, and while I ate, I congratulated myself on recognizing the gift of that moment, on slowing down and opening that particular box of joy. You see, I have a whole closet filled with unopened boxes of joy that I missed when my children were little because . . . well, my children were little. So, I was feeling very self-satisfied when Amanda passed by, making her sentry rounds, counting children, "one, two, three . . . where's four? Ah, four, five." She saw me in the castle eating and drinking, and I smiled and explained that, "When you are invited to have lunch with a princess in her castle, you should always say, "yes!" And that is good life advice because it's not every day that a princess shows up.

Interrupting our conversation, Anna looked up at me and said, "Nana, you never have to wait for an invitation. You can always come." Then, she nonchalantly resumed her cooking duties, unaware of the wonder of her words.

"You can always come." To be loved by a five-year-old is like nothing else on earth, and I still get a little misty-eyed when I remember the benediction she spoke over me. Because I had already accepted her invitation to share in her joy, I need not wait for another invitation to join her. I am always welcome. Her drawbridge is always open to me.

I heard another voice interwoven with Anna's. "Awara, you never need to wait for an invitation. You can always come to Me." I don't have to speak the magic words, or purchase a ticket, or even wait in line. And, this undoes me, this extravagant kindness, this unbounded generosity. At any moment, I can step into His presence, enter His kingdom, a kingdom which I, like Elisha's servant, cannot see (yet) even though I am surrounded by it. (2 Kings 6:17 NIV)

One of the reasons my grandchildren love this museum is that there is a room filled with costumes for them to wear, a miniature firefighter coat, a magician's cloak, multi-colored gowns, and jeweled crowns. And, when the Littles put on those royal robes and fight over who gets to sit on the child-sized throne, they are not pretending to be princes and princesses. They are practicing.

One day soon, all the sons and daughters of the King will reign with Him, and if you can understand that, I wish you would explain it to me.

If we have accepted His invitation to join Him in His kingdom and to sit at His table, get this, we never need to wait for another invitation before entering His presence. We all need to hear this truth, that we are welcome. Always. And, loved. So loved. And, safe. Forever safe, freed at last from the Curse. And, when this King shows up and invites you to enter into His presently, but not forever, invisible kingdom, to join Him for a feast, a meal for the ages as befits this Royal Host, you should always say "yes!"

The Wonder Years

By Nancy Carroll

I walk by dying dandelions every day. So common. Gone in a breath.

But when I take time to look, it's a magic moment. A lit sparkler. A wizard's wand. A glowing crown of thorns. A halo.

My husband and I are in our last quarter of life, what we've named our "Wonder Years." Yes. That can mean wondering where I put my phone, wondering how I'll not trip and fall, wondering what happened to my waist. But it is also the wonder of taking a deep breath to see a world that is filled with beauty, kindness, and miracles. Especially in a time that seems filled with ugliness, meanness, and despair. So instead of being ashamed of slowing down (it seems so un-American) we're trying to see it as a privilege. We get to stop and see, pause and point out, taste and relish.

All of life is holy.

If that is true—all of life is holy—why do I allow deadening distractions to snatch my attention away, and non-stop newsfeeds to magnify my fears, destroy my joy, and forget what's ahead?

"There will be a highway
called the Holy Road.
No one rude or rebellious
is permitted on this road.
It's for God's people exclusively—
impossible to get lost on this road.
Not even fools can get lost on it.
No lions on this road,
no dangerous wild animals—
Nothing and no one dangerous or threatening.
Only the redeemed will walk on it.
The people God has ransomed

will come back on this road.
They'll sing as they make their way home to Zion,
    unfading halos of joy encircling their heads,
Welcomed home with gifts of joy and gladness
    as all sorrows and sighs scurry into the night."

Isaiah 35:8-10 The Message

Think what awaits us because of the agonizing crown of thorns worn 2,000 years ago. **Unfading halos of joy** circling our heads, where all sorrows and sighs will scurry into the night.

Perhaps dandelions aren't common. They are signposts of what's to come. And as the breath of a breeze scatters the seeds, even more halos of joy will line that Holy Road to home.

Diatoms

By Tonia Stacey Gütting

In the blue water heart of the planet, a single-cell diatom goes about its merry business of breathing in carbon, breathing out oxygen and turning sunshine into food. His tiny life consists of little more than breathing, eating, and reproducing. But he does his job well, and my life depends on it.

His single-cell being cannot be seen by my eye, until he gets with a few bazillion of his buddies. That tends to happen when there's a rock concert—when the glaciers calve huge hunks, down-beating into the rippling blue-water heart with thunder-loud cracks and squawking-gull fans and people on boats adding the ooo's and ahhh's. It's the Woodstock for diatoms and they get all giddy and divide themselves into two and more until their blooming, burgeoning colony can be seen by humans, by radar, by space. The glacier flings a confetti of flour-dust full of iron, turning the water a turquoise blue. The diatoms scoop it up and flower into psychedelic bright green swirls.

After slamming a few glacial-flour beers and riding the crashing-ice roller coaster, the diatoms rise to the surface where there's more sun and they keep breathing—carbon in, oxygen out. You may have heard, like I did, that our oxygen comes from plants and especially great giant gargantuan trees of the rainforest where the toucan, capybara, and green iguana live and breathe. That is true. But only a little true. Most oxygen is from the tiny diatom in the waters of the world.

Actually, even the gargantuan Sumaumeira tree with its 10' diameter and 200' height appreciates the tiny diatom. When they die, their bodies drift to the bottom and when the waters dry up, like in the African Sahara desert, they become tiny pieces of sand. Then, when the Creator's winds blow, it carries those dead diatoms in clouds so big I can see them, radar can see them, space can see them. Those winds carry clouds of 27 million tons of diatom dust every year all the 1,600-miles way across the big water Atlantic and sprinkle it over the deep jungle as fertilizer which all those Sumaumeira trees need.

So when I have a big adrenaline day that crashes to a lonely night and my little insecurities grow into monstrous unproportionates and bring along their impossible irrational implausibilities masked as realities—that my children will hate me and my husband leave and I'll be destitute and alone for the rest of my single-being life and my mind spins that wheel of misfortune refusing to listen to rational words and my body fuels the fire all night long till at last with the dawn I can call my mom and tears come finally like rain in the storm but I still spend the day like a hollowed out shell and I can't breathe, not really, not deep as the cleansing waters for fear that the monsters will return—that's when I remember my little diatom friends and our big Abba God who made them, and me, and started our breaths. In. And out.

Imagine That

By Judy Swartz

"I have been crucified with Christ and I no longer live, but *Christ lives in me* (emphasis mine). The life I now live in the body, I live by faith in the Son of God, who loved me and gave Himself for me."[1]

God. Lives in me?

"Oh Happy Day"![2]

Move around in there, God.

Spread out.

Make plenty of room for yourself.

You are welcome here.

Forgive my audacity, but I've been a little busy with life lately.

Can I ask you to please clean up the place a bit while you're settling in?

It could really use some attention and I could really use the help.

My last tenant seemed so bent on destruction and clutter.

He wasn't very clean. He left messes everywhere. And he loved the dark.

He spent a good share of his time intricately weaving those cobwebs of lies you see hanging around in every corner.

Kinda like he wanted to ensure I would remain uncomfortable in my own skin.

Now that you're here, God, and he's gone, I am super anxious to sweep away all the dirt and wash away all the grime.

But God, we can't just leave it all empty and clean either.

I remember reading what Jesus told his disciples,

> When an impure spirit comes out of a person, it goes through arid places seeking rest and does not find it. Then it says, 'I will return to the house I left.' When it arrives, it finds the house unoccupied, swept clean and put in order.

---

1 Gal. 2:20 NIV

2 Wikipedia. 2024. "Oh Happy Day." Wikimedia Foundation. Last modified December 6, 2024. https://en.wikipedia.org/wiki/Oh_Happy_Day.

Then it goes and takes seven other spirits more wicked than itself, and they go in and live there. And the final condition of that person is worse than the first.[3]

I don't want that, God. I surely don't want that!
It's his turn to be told, "No room at the inn."[4]
I want you to fill this place up, God!
I want every trace of him removed as far as the east is from the west.[5]
Just like you said long ago, God, "Let there be light"![6]
Glimmering and shimmering light, casting rainbows of promise into every corner where those webs of lies were strung![7]
Rays of your love streaming in through every window!
I want to be full of life, God!
Deck the halls with boughs of goodness!
Slather the walls in whitewashed mercy!
Open the doors of peace, God. Shalom to all who enter and depart!
Let there be music! And Joy! And dancing!
Laughter, resounding from the rafters!
Hope, alive and breathing in every nook and cranny!
A well of purest living water overflowing for thirsty travelers to tarry for a time and refresh themselves.[8]
Vines bursting with an abundance of fresh fruit just waiting for a hungry soul to come along and pick some![9]
Eat and be filled with the Bread of Life.[10]
"O, taste and see that the Lord is good"![11]
The Lord is indeed, so very, very good!
Hang out our shingle, God: "This Establishment is Now Under New Management!"
And God, Thank you.
Thank you for coming into my mess.

---

3 Matt. 12:43-45 NIV
4 Luke 2:7 KJV
5 Ps. 103:12 NIV
6 Gen. 1:3 NIV
7 Gen. 9:13 NIV
8 John 7:38 NIV
9 John 15:5 NIV
10 John 6:35 NIV
11 Ps. 34:8 KJV

And thank you for helping me get it cleaned up.
I know I never could have done it without you, God.

All We Ever Really Need

By Theresa Miller

Is this it? Is this all there is? Laundry, dishes, and cleaning toilets; wiping bottoms, spills, and hand-rinsing soiled undergarments before tossing them into the washing machine, day after day?

And more repetitive than laundry and dishes is the ongoing task of disciplining and training hearts and minds that naturally bend toward self.

The job is never complete, and affirmation can seem non-apparent.

Yet, when I settle into the hard, mundane, and repetitive and accept it as my sacrifice, it becomes my joy.

Through the hard and mundane, it is the snuggles, giggles, and kisses goodnight, playfulness, laughter, and kindness that affirm me as a mother. And I delight in them.

I delight in watching my children splash, squeal, and cannonball right into the air-pumped pool on a hot summer day.

I delight in setting out chicken tenders and corn dogs for when they feel hungry and popsicles stashed in the cooler with ice.

I delight in creating opportunities for my children and watching them grow.

I delight in the moments I can sit back and inhale who they are becoming.

I receive these affirmations daily when I open my eyes to see.

And if I ever want more out of life, I have learned to look no further than what is right before me. I have learned to travel not farther but deeper to see all there is—seeking greater love, gratitude, and joy in the here and now.

Because this is it, these are the moments that matter.

At the heart of washing clothes, dishes, and bottoms is devotion, and at the heart of discipline and training is belief.

And that is all we ever really need.

The Coat My Mother Chose

By Marilyn R. Gardner

My mom raised five children between worlds, navigating between her missionary life in Pakistan and furloughs in the United States. The latter were seasons meant for rest but often brought their own unique stresses. Among those challenges was learning how to parent from a distance while we were in boarding school and how to recalibrate when we all came home. When I became a mom, I looked back on moments from my childhood with wonder, marveling at how she managed it all. That wonder is sometimes laced with laughter, and other times, it carries a poignant nostalgia.

Every year as the weather changes, replacing hot sunny summers with cold fall winds, I think back on a memory from my teenage years that captures my mom's ability to navigate what was often a rough parenting journey. It's a story about buying a coat, a seemingly benign and ordinary act that paints a powerful picture of parental love and patience.

When I was fourteen years old, we were on a furlough from Pakistan living next to my Grandma K and cousins in a small town in Central Massachusetts. I was not a nice 14-year-old. I was out of my habitat and missing my small boarding school in the foothills of the Himalayas. I struggled with my identity. Who was I outside of Pakistan? *What* was I? I knew I wasn't Pakistani, but I sure didn't feel American. I didn't know how to describe the life I had come from when asked, and I struggled with my friendships, especially missing my best friend, who had entered her sophomore year in high school back in Pakistan. Worst of all, I struggled with my weight. It is not an exaggeration to say that I ate all my feelings in the form of hot dogs, occasional Mc-Donald's Big Macs, and gourmet peppermint ice cream enjoyed on Sunday nights when we would travel home from any of New

England's small Baptist churches. As if all this wasn't enough, I was dreadfully out of fashion. This is not just my imagination. Pictures from the past are proof beyond my memory, showing an awkward teen and equally awkward clothing.

I was not the only one feeling out of her depth. Along with the cross-cultural adjustments of parenting, my mom was struggling to keep her kids fed and clothed on a missionary's salary. All these variables met together through a coat. As the leaves fell and the weather grew colder, the light windbreaker I was wearing was no longer adequate for the frosty November mornings. I needed a winter coat, and I needed it soon.

American shopping with my mom was not a favorite or comfortable activity for either of us. We were used to the chaos of busy bazaars where multicolored and textured fabrics lined the walls, and we were served tea as we picked out bolts of cloth for dresses, shirts, and pants. In this case, necessity trumped comfort, and we arranged to shop for a coat on a weekday. The plan was for my mom to pick me up after school and drive to a store a half hour away. I was sullen as we drove out of the high school parking lot. It was cold, far colder than the winters in Pakistan that I was used to, where palm trees swayed in cool mornings and the sun burned off early morning mist, making midday warm and comfortable. This was New England, and the leaves had long left the trees, readying for winter's long slumber. Beyond the cold, I wanted to be with my friends, and I knew, I just knew we wouldn't find a coat to suit me.

What I didn't know was that my mom had been at the store we were going to earlier that day and had found a coat. It was the latest style - brown/beige plaid, double-breasted with big brown buttons. It was my size, and it was on sale. She was brimming with delight and wonder at this extraordinary find. There was only one catch. Given my life stage, my mom knew that if she bought the coat Band brought it home, my response would be an emphatic "I hate this coat!" just to spite her. It took her only a moment to make up her mind. She would hide it among the other coats and pray to the God who counts the hairs on our heads, the God who lives between worlds, and surely must understand the struggles of a parent who loves their child even through their worst stages. She hid the coat as best she could and went on with her day. I would know none of this until years later.

My mom picked me up as planned, and we headed straight to the winter coat section when we arrived at the store. There were beautiful coats in cream, brown, and beige—all made of wool, with an elegant look and price tags to match. On another rack were the more affordable options, which looked, well, cheaper. I was aware of the prices as I angrily sifted through the coats I liked on the expensive rack. My mom watched me for a moment and then, noticing my frustration, pulled out the coat she had set aside earlier. I took it from her, trying to mask my excitement, and casually slipped it on in front of the full-length mirror. It was perfect—like it had been made just for me. In the reflection, I saw my 14-year-old self, wrapped in a stylish design that hid imperfections and revealed a young woman with clear skin and a hint of newfound confidence. I smiled at the girl in the mirror and inadvertently at the mother standing behind her.

"Oh Marilyn! It's lovely!" My mom's voice was a bit shaky. "Do you like it?" "Yes," I responded. "Do you want to look at any others?" She asked, not wanting to push her luck. No, I didn't. It was the right coat at the right price. We carried it up to the front and paid for it. "That's a beautiful coat! And on sale too!" said the cashier approvingly. She kept it on the hanger, placing it carefully into a bag. Outside, the November sun was setting, and the air was chillier. Lights were going on in the dimming light as people wrapped up their days, readying to head home for the evening.

We didn't say much on the way home. We didn't need to. Thinking back, my mom must have felt gratefully triumphant. What could have been a difficult, if not disastrous, shopping trip turned into a successful and memorable time. The ride home was still quiet, but the tension was absent, teenage sullenness replaced by comfortable hope.

Parenting is full of the unexpected. There are times when we've got it, we are parenting in ways that make us feel pretty great, in ways that clearly demonstrate our love for our kids and their responses to that love. There are other times where the pain and frustration are overwhelming, where the babies that came into our lives as dictators have now become anarchists, and we are so done. Anger flares. Mean things are sometimes said, and we hate ourselves for saying them. We are desperately afraid that as much as we love them, we don't love them enough. Then there are those moments when we ache over what our kids are feeling and experiencing. We long to be able to speak love and affirmation into the hard spaces, letting them know they are beloved by us and by God. We want to tell the chubby teen in front of us that they are beautiful, that what is seen is a fraction of the whole, that ducklings turn into swans or maybe not, but we and the God we love care infinitely for them, love them, and are amazed at the beauty of who they are at their core. But we find ourselves blocked by our inability to convey what we long to, and even when we do, disheartened by kids who are locked into their own insecurity, bent on discouraging any movement forward.

As I look back at my 14-year-old self and the memorable coat that made me look as chic as a young teen can look, I'm reminded of my mom and all the "coat" moments that come with parenting, moments that were a part of her life and later became a part of mine. In that miracle coat moment, all the world was made right between a teenager and her mom. At least until the next morning.

My mom died in November of 2023. As I remember this story, I remember my mom and I feel the loss. The loss of a parent who finds a coat and hides it in the rack for a teenager bent on refusing overtures of love. The loss of a mom who loves unconditionally through the hard and good things in life, offering a model of how I can do the same.

Learning to See Beyond the Familiar

By Sarah K. Butterfield

The top of the stairs at the edge of Sunset Cliffs is the best beach view in all of San Diego. The palm trees sway to the salty wind up above, the surfers catch waves down below, and the glittering water meets sand and rocky cliffs as far as the eye can see. I've walked down these steep stairs too many times to count over the years, usually in late winter, when the tide is low during the daytime and when staring at the horizon might reveal whales spouting water. I descend with my hopes high: What will we find in the tide pools today?

When our boys were little, they would point out hermit crabs with their chubby fingers and watch them crawl across the rocks, delighted by their miniature alien bodies halfway out of their shells. Once, a kind stranger drew our attention to a dark purple blob, a fat sea slug known as a Sea Hare, and we watched it inch along the tide pool. We picked it up gently and took turns holding it, marveling over its squishy body. And I can still hear the squeals of delight the day my husband flipped over a large rock halfway submerged in the water, to reveal a family of Brittle Sea Stars. These creatures have a round disc in the center of their body with several thin, snake-like arms that help them move quickly. Whether they are tiny or bigger than the palm of my hand, it's a thrill to hold them.

Now that our boys are gangly tweens, we still love coming to the tide pools, but I admit that familiarity has dulled the experience. We hardly give the hermit crabs a second glance. We're glad to find the Brittle Sea Stars, but we don't need to hold them anymore. The Sea Hares have become more and more elusive and require more patience to spot than we sometimes have. These days, our eyes sweep past the common sea anemones in search of something novel to impress us.

When we come to expect the glorious, it ceases to amaze us. Our beloved tide pools have become so familiar to us that it is only when we encounter the unexpected that our hearts are filled with wonder. This often feels like a gift: a pod of dolphins leaping in and out of the waves just beyond the shore, or a squadron of pelicans swooping down near us. More often than not, it takes effort to uncover awe, like when my husband flipped over dozens of ordinary-looking rocks to discover an abalone shell, its iridescence glinting in the evening sun. Or when our persistence and patience led us to our very first octopus sighting, its tentacles unfurling as it tried to hide underneath a rock.

We worship the God of the unexpected. God is the one who sewed clothes for Adam and Eve in the middle of their worst moment. God is the one who spoke through a burning bush, a common donkey, a gentle whisper in the wind. God chose the little brother over and over. God brought victory in battle with tiny armies, and with one well-aimed rock. But we have become so familiar with these stories that our eyes glide over the words, missing God's glory in the unexpected.

The gospels are full of people who are "amazed" at Jesus's teachings and miracles—when he healed the sick, cast out demons, calmed the storm, answered hard questions, foretold his death and resurrection. The women were amazed at the empty tomb, and the two followers on their way to Emmaus were "astounded" at the women's testimony (Luke 24:22-23, NRSV). Jesus is beckoning us to be amazed as well, to marvel at what God is like and what God has done. This can be difficult for those of us who grew up in church, who have heard the Bible stories time and again.

What would it take for us to recover a sense of wonder at what God is doing, both in the pages of Scripture and in our daily lives? We can start by doing three things.

1. Slow Down

Let's linger with the words when we open our Bibles, picking shorter passages and reading them several times. Let's pay attention to what's grabbing our attention. When we go slow, we have the time to ask wondering questions, to consider the context, to muse about what the passage might be telling us about what God is like.

Just as important is to slow down in our daily lives. When we stop cramming our days so full and build in some margin, we will then have the ability to go slow to notice the truth, beauty, and goodness all around us, and to respond to the people crossing our path with love. We can take a minute to marvel, to recenter our attention on our loving Creator.

2. Cultivate Patience and Persistence

It's easy for our eyes to skip past a passage of text we don't understand or to ignore troubling questions when we encounter difficult verses. But if we can be patient and persistent, checking commentaries or Bible dictionaries or other people who have wrestled with the text, there is treasure to be found. Spiritual growth often happens through discomfort, which is why it's better to persist in patience than to avoid altogether.

When we are ready to focus our eyes on wonder in our daily lives, we must also be patient and persistent. We live in a world of instant gratification, and we can easily become discouraged if at first we don't find what we're looking for. Instead of giving up, practice staying open. Keep watch even in the most mundane moments, and remember that abalone shells look like regular rocks until they're flipped upside down.

3. Develop Humility

If we are to be amazed at what God is like and what God has done within the pages of Scripture, we must approach the text in a posture of humility. Viewing the Bible as a book of answers filled with knowable facts instead of the mysterious, inspired text that it is strips it of its life-changing power. But when we come to it with open minds and humble hearts, using our biblical imagination and reading in context, we are more likely to meet God anew within its pages.

In the same way, when we approach the world around us with humility, acknowledging the limits of our understanding and developing a sense of curiosity, we can make room for wonder. In our age of instant information, there is plenty of room for discovery. This is true of our interactions with other people, too—humility leads to listening, which leads to compassion, which leads to the wonders of love.

When I stand at the top of the steep stairs of Sunset Cliffs, overlooking the tide pools below, I am reminded that to live as the people of God is to live as wonder-filled people. May our every step through Scripture and through life be filled with amazement.

When Lois Ann Wakes Up

By Abigail Hofland

Lois Ann always wakes up to the unknown. She doesn't recognize the paintings on her wall. She is unsure whether to get out of bed or turn over for a few more hours of sleep. Her sense of time has dissipated as her years have increased and her mind has weakened.

This morning, Lois Ann gets up. Her fire-red pixie cut is uncombed, unwashed. The dye is too scarlet to appear natural. It doesn't matter. She loves red. Lois Ann chooses a summery outfit. The spring day is chilly and crisp, but to Lois Ann it is always summer. I once watched her don shades and shorts to sunbathe from a rocking chair in November.

"I love the sun," she had said. "The wind can go take a hike."

Moments after stepping outside her room, Lois Ann stands at my desk with a smile bolder than her mane. I see that she found her purple lipstick.

"Good morning, Lois Ann!"

"Good morning!" she bursts out laughing. "Is it morning? Did I miss lunch?"

Before I can respond, she looks around the lobby area of our Senior Living community and gasps.

"This place! I can't get over this place!" she says. "Those pillows are beautiful!" she gestures toward the couch. "And I love your hair! I wish I had hair like that. Are you going to have a baby?"

She notices my third trimester bump. She doesn't remember that she has watched my baby grow since day one. It doesn't matter. She's watching now.

"Yes, our first. We can't wait."

"Is it going to be a little boy or a little girl?" she leans in with interest, eyes widening.

"We're not finding out! We like surprises."

"Maybe you'll have twins. I'm a twin. My poor mother," she laughs and tells me she loves my hair. She wishes she had hair like that. What day is it? Is it morning? What beautiful pillows! She loves this place. Am I going to have a baby?

Every day, Lois Ann revels in the novelty of the familiar. It could be that her ever shortening memory necessitates this, but memory loss is not always redeemed by those who journey through it. Many of Lois Ann's peers are aware of their cognitive decline. Some visit the front desk to complain about cold soup. Lois Ann has bid farewell to more cognitive functioning than any of her friends. She only complains when it's too cold to pick flowers.

"I love flowers. I just *love* them," she stomps her foot for emphasis, throws her head back, and laughs. "And I found these. I can't *believe* I found them. Right there! I was just walking, and I looked down, and *boom*. These."

It is afternoon now. She holds up a bouquet of roses from one of our landscaped bushes. Some people don't notice we have those bushes. Lois Ann discovers them every day.

"Have you ever seen a pink like this before?"

She thrusts the bouquet in my face and lets me feel the petals. Lois Ann demands experiential awe. She places palm to forehead and shakes her head, speechless. "Beautiful. I'm going to take these to my room. Which way is my room?"

I tell her. My baby kicks, and I place a hand on the bump. Lois Ann rediscovers it. Delight erupts. She floods me with the same questions she has asked every day for the past seven months. She tells me motherhood will be the greatest blessing in my life. Though she struggles to recall the number of children she has, Lois Ann never forgets the joy of being a mother.

Motherhood is already a blessing for me. Another is to carry a child into the temporal world as I work with people who are aging into the eternal. We all live on eternity's brink as much as our babies and seniors, but these groups embody a paradox of weakness and strength, ever reminding us what it's like to wake up.

The Witness of a Penny

By Nikki Hurt

Like a prologue to their own story, the six shiny pennies sat nestled together in my father's pocket as he walked along the sidewalk with my mother. This was on the occasion of their third meeting; but before a third meeting can occur, a second, and of course a first, have to happen.

It was the fall of 1969. Having grown up on the west side of South Bend, Indiana my dad was a proud Washington Panther. Washington was having a stellar year in football and the Panthers would go on to win the mythical championship that season. Mythical—for all the non-football fanatics—because it pre-dated an official high school playoff which wouldn't arrive on the scene in Indiana until the mid 70s. Therefore, officials would pronounce a mythical championship to the team that had the best record. As 1969 came to an end, South Bend Washington would be declared the top team of their class for Indiana football.

Sensing the excitement that was to come from the game, my dad, Charles Kaufman, (or Chuck to everyone who knew him) agreed to let his friend, Larry, pick him up for the game that night in Elkhart. The trip was taken in Larry's bright orange Studebaker Lark. A beloved vehicle that Larry had restored and painted his choice of a vibrant orange hue.

Chuck, Larry, and the bright orange Lark pulled into the parking lot of Rice Field that Friday night in 1969 with the boys hoping to see their team pull one out against the defending champions of the year before—The Blue Blazers of Elkhart Central.

As the guys climbed through the stands that October Friday night, the lights of the football field lighting their path among the crowd of people in the stands, Chuck's eyes settled upon a young woman whom he had never seen before. Dressed in a red trench coat and matching pants, Renee Ewing from Jackson High in South Bend, came to the game with her best friend, Debbie.

Debbie was Chuck's favorite art room classmate at Washington; she had talked a bit about Renee as the two friends drew with their chalk pencils over the wide black desktops of the art room. My dad later confessed to me that it was in the art room where he found his confidence. Not only in his amazing art ability but also in his relationships with the opposite sex. Having been a quiet young man, he was used to being picked on, maybe even bullied, by other male classmates; but here, in the art room, conversation was easier to be had than in other areas of high school. There was a lot of time to talk as they drew and painted and my dad grew in his artistic ability as well as his conversational confidence in chatting with his beautiful classmates.

He saw Renee among the crowd at Rice Field, and knew immediately she was the girl that Debbie had so often mentioned. He noticed her feminine figure in the stunning red coat with the matching red pants, but they didn't actually speak. He also noticed she was wearing a wig (yes, a wig—a rage for all the young women at that time) and he wondered what her hair looked like underneath. He wondered about her a lot. How could he have known this would be the woman who would become his wife and the mother of his 3 children? He was just a sophomore at a football game at Rice Field in October of 1969 and it would be months until they would meet again and he would have the courage to speak to her.

Scene change to the second meeting.

Nearly nine months later, he had his chance to speak to her when sitting in his high school cafeteria to pick up his yearbook—he saw her. Walking amongst them in her blue dress, red ribbons adorning her dark brown hair (the real thing this time), along with red, white, and blue sandals—she was the patriotic muse of his dreams. She had come to tag along with her friend, Debbie while she also picked up her yearbook and chatted with school friends.

This time, they said hello.

This time, they shook hands.

That could have been the end of their association, but it wasn't.

Final scene change—the third meeting.

It was the spring of his junior year, nearly a year had passed since he shook the hand of the girl in blue and spoke his hello. He had been invited by Debbie to spend the afternoon with some of her friends...*yes, Renee will be here.*

He stood, waiting for the door to be answered and nervously tampered with the six pennies he suddenly noticed in the pocket of his Levi's.

The day would end beautifully. Many years later, we learned that he kissed her in a closet—thanks to the scheming of Debbie's younger sister who shoved them in it together. On the day it was revealed to us, she would be morbidly embarrassed that their secret was out, but we—her children and grandchildren—rolled with laughter upon learning it. Did they escape from a Beach Blanket Bingo teen movie or did real teenagers in the 1970s actually meet their boyfriends this way?

He went home that night, determined not to let months go by without seeing her, emptied his pockets and realized—*the pennies were shining.*

Growing up, I knew my dad carried change in his pocket every day. I recall him coming home after work and emptying it into a change drawer on the top of his dresser. It was a rote routine set against the backdrop of my childhood and it held no meaning.

To me.

Had I paid closer attention to the collection I would have seen them there all along—the six shiny pennies he carried every day without fail. Intent on keeping the shine, he occasionally switched out the duller ones for new ones that still held their gleam.

This weekend we will gather as a family to celebrate their union which has now lasted 50 years. My father will arrive, likely holding the hand of my mother, and as he walks up the front steps of the lake house—Listen closely.

Do you hear?

The faint jingle of change; a testament to the day our family, ordained by God, sparked into existence—they're here, nestled in his pocket holding their shine and bearing witness to it all.

Moonshadow

By Civil Winters

There would be no rain. I wrung my hands together and begged beneath the cloudless sky. It opened its mouth, relentlessly blue and unforgivingly endless. Nothing spilled out. In a last-ditch effort, I slid my dusty feet into my finest wellingtons and glibly danced an unceremonial water jig. This weary plea for something of measure to pour from the heavens—scant or sacred, rotund or willing—was rewarded with further scorch and silence. Not one delicious, decided drop dripped down onto the heads of the thirsting grain. Awns outstretched and browning stems crinkled over, it looked as if the stunted western red spring wheat was also kneeling in surrender to the clime. The heat wafted carelessly by, turning the kernels away, watching them shrivel. Begrudgingly, I stuffed myself back into overheated work shoes and resumed digging in the crusted clay.

This summer was particularly ruthless. It was the hottest, driest period Manitoba had experienced in over 100 years. It began in deficit, as there had been little precipitation the entire preceding season. Forest and grassland species alike responded in stress. An overabundance of cones was formed by the blue and white spruce, and the cottonwoods blew their pearly tufts ahead of schedule. Sandbar willow, boxelder maple, and scrub oak sentinels stood, their outerwear wrinkled and lusterless and ready to shed before autumn. The hardy tallgrass prairie perennials were spent, channelling whatever energy they could muster into multiplying their seed heads to scatter.

Local farmers were beyond middling concern that crop failure was on the horizon. Their fear for yield was not beyond reason. Thirty-degree days spanned the length of summer without a single break in the sky. Throughout June to August, some regions received as little as 0.8 inches of rain. Other areas received even less. Many growers culled, portioned or liquidated their cattle herds due to unavailable feed and unsustainable expenses.

Without knowing an extreme drought was in the forecast, this planting and design season was one of the most crucial and intense I have ever experienced. There were both large public spaces to maintain as well as personal ones. Each was in its infancy. In regenerative agriculture, seedlings are willingly exposed to harsh terrain, wild edges, and competition. The success of a fresh planting in these landscapes is both limited *by* and dependent *upon* the availability of water.

In April, I observed on tenterhooks as the spring melt vanished rapidly. No run-off was left to renew the parched groundwater. Any tender slips—tree, bush or perennial—would not endure the spring or summer without a constant and watchful eye. This moment marked the beginning of a tumultuous long-term relationship with 500 feet of industrial grade watering hose.

Right foot leading, I hovered above the step of my shovel. With vengeance directed towards the maniacal sun, I swiftly pressed the serrated edge below. The hard, greying earth, once sumptuous and lush in tone, crunched and repelled. It would not give.

I looked down at the trays of unsown plugs. Whorled milkweed, purple prairie clover, and gumweed stared upwards expectantly in the light. Swaths of stiff and showy goldenrod leaned impatiently on the marginally arid side. Moisture oriented varieties, the sweet flag, crow's foot violet, and marsh marigold, were beginning to wither. They would require root soaking before placement in the soil. I hadn't reached the warm and cool season grasses, or the Campfire roses and Morden Snow potentillas beyond.

My brain scrambled to recall the last top-up in this section. In the climbing temperatures, it was unreasonable to ask a new planting to exist without a fresh, near-daily drink. Unlike the rain, the workload was torrential. Daylight waned and everything was thirsty, but there was too much ground left to cover to break for tea.

Checking the weekly watering schedule, I performed a little "gardener math" to calculate how many species I could reach before dusk. With 2 to 10 minutes of watering required per plant,

variety and size dependent, tending another 100 plants before dark was a pipe dream. I tucked my beloved long-handle shovel to the side and picked up the end of the fireman's nozzle. If I dragged the hose towards the end of the acreage and set my timer, I could ensure the newest area was addressed before tomorrow's responsibilities demanded their due.

As I connected the last length of hose, I reflected on this year's desperate cry *for* and utter lack *of* water. Although it is regarded as a symbol of tranquility and resilience, it had become the bane of my existence. A sharp pang of guilt accompanied this admission, knowing I should be grateful for *access* to running water. I did not mean this flippantly.

In the midst of the bitter recent winter, my family's well pump had self-destructed. We spent seven weeks without water. Absolutely nothing, from washing machine to taps, functioned between February and April. We relied entirely on support to fill and deliver portable containers to our rural domicile. Unsure of when or how water would be functional again, every seed started in the frigid cold was sustained by the care of a neighbour's hand.

Other areas of life were undergoing scarcity alongside. Caretaking, cancer, addiction, betrayal, and a slipping sense of self loomed, an unpredictable weather pattern. Although only a handful of these variables had names then, the effects were winding together. They would become a tremendous, uncontrollable later dust bowl.

I slung the links over my shoulder to drag the hose again. Sweat dripped down my neck, attracting a blur of flea beetles. The dry conditions had given them free reign over the crop, and they welcomed this opening with devastation. This was meant to be the time of bud and bloom. These were months for turning my hands over and again within the tilth of the black prairie chernozemic soil. No signs of amazement persisted here, no indication of living water. There was only a perpetual wasteland. Following the loops of the hose, checking for snags, I felt like Ouroboros chasing my tail. Unlike the myth, this repetitive devouring left little room to imagine greening. It seemed as if beauty would never return.

It was after 10pm when I reached the end of my charge. Flipping the nozzle to *off*, I pulled the hoses towards their final destination. My shovel dominant leg protested, and tiny clods of earth were strewn between my teeth. It would require a spool of dental floss to remedy, but I could only dream of washing the day down with milky earl grey.

That is when it happened. Small against the evening and hovered over the faucet, something peculiarly rough and wrinkled grazed the top of my head. I leapt away, hopping madly in search for the prankster responsible. No admission was detected. *"Labouring under the sky must have addled my brain"* I thought, and returned to the outlet. Again, the sensation of gnarled sandpaper slid rudely across my hair.

Gardeners are acclimatized to looking down, tiptoeing to edges and searching between lines to capture what is unnoticed. In the full, round glow of the August Sturgeon Moon, I chose to look *up*. Mirrored beneath that face was another face, pale and heart shaped.

A barn owl. I had never seen one, but the buff grey and rust patina of her body spoke immediately. Her underwings reflected nocturnal tidings as she unfurled them to their full breadth. Her fore-feathers flickered, teasing the southeast wind. It was the vessel she undoubtedly arrived on, an infrequent visitor far from her home. The *woosh* as she passed was enchanting. She lingered in course, her obsidian eyes meeting mine as she retracted her talons. In one lilting motion, she nudged and drew my face into the midnight sky. A smile unfolded. We gathered in it equally. I stood in admiration, and she observed, head-turned until the breeze beckoned her farther out.

She visited, an offbeat rhythm, throughout the following year. She dove out of treelines on walks, cutting across my path in a speckled twist. She passed over fields as I witnessed stalks ripple like the tide. Then, in a silent, exiting current, she went.

Summer's sweltering sentence had been paused with astonishment. Without the heaviness of this chapter—the earth moving and the boundless shuffling of a watering hose—would this moment have existed? I will never know. In the highest of temperatures in the lowest of seasons, however, awe swooped in.

"Did it take long to find me?"[1] I asked as the owl flew overhead, softening into her shadow on the moon. There had been no designated search. Still, she had arrived like the reprieve that comes with a milder, changing forecast. Tomorrow, the to-do list would call, and watering would start again. I would continue to steward the spaces where I was setting roots. Tonight, though? Tonight, I would soar with a barn owl, and witness as delight softened a calloused heart.

____

1 "Moonshadow," Cat Stevens, Teaser and the Firecat, A&M, 1971

The Wonder of Silent Letters and Spider-Man

by Ashley Setterlind

My pastor is 22 minutes into his sermon. He is preaching on the collision of grace and forgiveness, a topic I need reminding of often. I'm recording additional reflections in my notebook like the pen in my hand might suddenly disintegrate if I don't write fast enough—as if the train of thought may pass by without first collecting me, an eagerly awaiting passenger.

My stream of consciousness vanishes with a soft *tap, tap, tap* on my shoulder. "Mommy," my second-born whispers, "why does my name start with a K if it doesn't make a *'kuh'* sound?" I turn, bewildered at the timing of his question. "That's a great question to ask, buddy. I love your curiosity. Let's talk about it after church, okay?" I answer softly.

Momentarily satisfied by my response, my son goes back to coloring the Spider-Man picture in front of him, using only the blue crayon—his favorite. I smile and chuckle to myself, reminded by his simple question that my baby boy is now more 'boy' than 'baby.' I think back to when my husband and I named him, and how we pondered the futuristic day when he might ask this very question. We considered the complicated phonetics of a silent letter from the viewpoint of a five-year-old learning alphabet sounds in preparation for reading. We joked about this imaginary conundrum as expectant parents. We acknowledged how to us, it would be insignificant, and he would just...learn. We also shared the realization that names are formative to the human soul, and we vowed to do our part in making our children feel deeply seen and known. This question, a part of the fabric of my son's very being, would be handled with care. Now, that day had arrived.

How can we possibly be here already? Like every other mother in the history of the universe, I can't stop my heart from aching over time's thievery. I marvel at the bitter sting of nostalgia, how it ignites my nervous system with a primal desperation to hold him in my arms once again, to drink him in, to rememorize the way his eyelashes fluttered closed with contentment at my nourishment and how he used to squeal with delight and dancing at the introduction to Mickey Mouse Clubhouse. Tears appear unannounced as I remember it all in flashes: the utter exhaustion, the unseen battle with depression, the unacceptable moments of sinful rage, the unexpected difficulty of raising two under two, and the truly unbridled joy of being called "mama."

My perspective is different now as a mother of four earthside babies, plus one in heaven. As I look at the beautiful young boy sitting at my feet, I consider his baby brother in the nursery down the hall, still fresh and new and innocent and lovely. I beg God to forgive me again for the moments I've squandered, asking him to renew my strength so that I might remain present for all the fleeting moments yet to come. As I believe he already has, I realize the greater question is: can I forgive myself? I recognize the voice of condemnation creeping in again. *You didn't enjoy them enough, and now it's too late. You missed it, too concerned with your temporary to-do list; too preoccupied by your pain to fully live. They'll never be that little ever again. This is your last chance with the final baby. You have to be better, healthier, more capable of holding. it. ALL.*

One word gently rises above the spiraling internal dialogue: **grace**. I sense that though I heard my pastor's audible voice, the Holy Spirit was speaking. *You were never meant to hold it all, dear one*, he says. *That's my job.*

Forgiveness, motherhood, and receiving honest questions from a developing critical thinker: all gifts of grace. None of it deserved. None of it earned by merit. None of it achieved with a sense of finality.

I'm not good enough to atone for my own sin. His grace for forgiveness is sufficient. I'm not faithful enough to be the parent I want to be all the time. His grace for motherhood is sufficient. I'm not patient enough, compassionate enough, or wise enough to answer every child's questions honorably. His grace for instruction and the formation of character is sufficient.

Why should I think I am enough to sustain that which I am not enough to give in the first place? Bearing this weight of responsibility is foolishness, particularly for the one who serves Christ. I am approved by his blood; not my ambition. I am accepted by his love; not my list of accomplishments. He desires that I rest in the richness of that unconditional, unwavering love.

Motherhood requires faith. Faith that our children will grow up to be kind, honest, and confident in their worth as human beings created by the God who loved them from before the beginning of time. Faith that they will not be forever scarred by our parenting blunders, but end up desiring a continued relationship with us.

Forgiveness is formed in faith. Faith to believe that we can trust God's perfect justice, even when we don't see evidence of every wrong righted on this side of eternity. Faith to celebrate that such is the case, for we know the burden of our own mistakes as it is.

And grace. Well, grace comes *through* faith. It is the gift of God, not formed by works, so that we may not boast apart from boasting in his character. What a wonder: to live this story in real time. What grace, to have breath in our lungs at all; to be a mother at all; to be forgiven at all; to have faith at all.

So may we live in wonder.

By God's grace.

In light of his mercy.

Forgiven and forgiving.

Explaining silent letters to not-so-silent baby boys.

Basking in baskets of blue artwork.

Full of awe for it all.

A Magical Moment

By M.L. Cole

Late one afternoon, I was absentmindedly washing strawberries at the kitchen sink, and peering out the window into our backyard. There were dozens of birds foraging in the grass, made up of several different species, landing here and fluttering there. Off to the side, a squirrel was busy digging in the ground, looking for food on the somewhat blustery day. Back behind the hostas and under the peonies, baby bunnies that were born in our yard late that summer were playing hide and seek, before bouncing off toward the arborvitae trees.

Seeing all of these creatures together was almost surreal, like this little woodland festival taking place just outside the window. Of course I've seen all these animals before, but rarely all in a single frame, just perfectly content, living out their lives alongside one another. Something about it made me so happy and filled with awe, to witness the most natural moment yet filled with such whimsy and inspiration.

I ran to grab my phone and take a quick video, thinking surely no one would believe me or understand just how miraculous it looked without evidence. But mere seconds later, when I returned to the window, they were ALL gone—every last one of them, and I couldn't help but laugh in disbelief. Not a single creature was left on the lawn or in nearby trees, like all of them had been part of some cosmic escape plan.

Being a writer, I resorted to journaling about it instead. In the moment, it was minorly frustrating, but also an ironically beautiful lesson to simply enjoy life as it comes, rather than trying to preserve every last detail. Words can't perfectly capture the magic of that moment... but neither could a photo or video. Don't get me wrong, there is incredible writing and exquisite photography out there, but human means can never fully encapsulate the glory of God's creation unfolding right before us.

I think that's something we all need to be reminded of from time to time, whether you're an artist or not. So let this silly yet profound moment be encouragement to live more of this life in the present, where God graciously created us to reside.

Offering Up Our Ordinary

How God's Delight in Our Work Transforms Our
Weariness into Wonder

by Mckenzie Hunt

The monitor flashes in the dark. A cry cuts through my bleary dream and I pry open my sleep-swollen eyes to the pitch-black room, confused. It's not yet dawn. But my daughter is awake. Again.

Peeling my skin from the warmth of the sheets, I look at the time on my phone and groan. *Why now?*

Stumbling to the stairs, my hand finds the railing in the dark and pulls the seemingly leaden rest of me up to the second floor nursery. There she stands, clinging to the spindles on her wooden crib like the bars of a prison cell. "Jailbird Jane" we sometimes call her during the day, smiling at her full-bodied expectancy. But it's *slightly* harder to feel endeared at 5 AM when all you want is to be back in the warmth of your bed.

She refuses the bottle. A quick sniff tells me her diaper is clean. I press my hand to her forehead but it's cool to the touch. *So why are you awake?* I think through clenched teeth.

With all the force of her 14 months of strength, she thrusts her arm to the bookshelf beside us and grabs her recent favorite, *Goodnight Gorilla*. And there I have my answer: this dear and insatiably inquisitive child woke before dawn, ravenous for one thing and one thing alone: *to be read out loud to.*

***

Motherhood is all at once a wondrous and wearisome thing. Full of countless moments like these. Moments, both tender and tiresome, that can sometimes feel like one long blur of our childrens' needs. And how, I wonder, am I to see these moments? These 5 AM readings? As exasperating or endearing? As golden opportunities or a loss of precious sleep?

At the heart of these questions lies a central doubt that, some days, as a mom, I wrestle with hourly. *Does it matter?* The picking up the Legos before breakfast when you know they'll be strewn across the floor again before lunch? The tenth diaper you've wrestled onto those kicking legs today? The laundry that no one sees (or seems to remember) that you fold? In the steady stream of seemingly insignificant tasks, we can wonder about the significance of our lives. Especially when the hours and laundry loads are passed in obscurity.

Yet it's not only in motherhood that I've asked these questions, but in all the ordinary and sometimes less-than-glamorous callings of my day-to-day life. And I know they don't just apply to the stay-at-home-mom life because they are the same questions that have followed me from when I was a student to when I worked full-time; from job to job, and from life stage to life stage. And I believe they all boil down to one question: *do the unsung moments of our ordinary days matter?* All the homework you stayed late in the classroom grading; all the charts you pored over long before your first patient of the day; all of that endless onslaught of meal prepping and laundry and dishwasher loads. *Does it matter?* We have wondered wearily, at the end of so many days.

Without a way of seeing the value in the seemingly trivial and unseen work of our daily lives, life begins to feel like an altogether wearisome task. Like a heavy burden we bear. Like yet another night of lost sleep that has been taken from me.

But what if there were another way to see the seemingly insignificant moments we spend in obscurity?

For whatever reason, one year I decided to go above and beyond to celebrate my husband's birthday. I sent invitations far and wide and bought cartloads of food. I baked and cooked and decorated all week, even painted a banner and hand-constructed party games. And this on top of my already busy caseload at work. But I remember how thrilling it all felt, how whimsical and exhilarating—running errands, decorating the apartment, bacon-wrapping the dates, piping frosting on the cake. I remember, distinctively, the feeling of delighting in every tiny task.

And why?

Because I love Matthew and loved the moment of seeing the delight in his eyes, his surprised smile, surrounded by friends in the glow of candles arranged on the Oreo cheesecake I learned, just for him, how to bake. I basked in his joy like a flower unfurling in the sun, like leaves drinking in rain. And in that moment, between delight dawning on his face and cutting the cake, it struck me: *What if I did everything in my life like I was throwing God a party?*

What if all of my work—all the trivial tasks and unsung errands, all the sleepless nights and too-long days—could feel like this? Like I was doing it for someone I so deeply loved because I could hardly wait to see the smile on their face? The delight dawn in their wonder-struck eyes?

This, I have come to believe, is the very thing that equips us to embrace rather than weary of all that seems trivial and insignificant in our day-to-day lives. It is the practice of offering it all—every dish, every diaper, every too-long commute—up to our Heavenly Father. Taking up each task, like my preparations for my husband's birthday, as a tiny but very real way to delight his heart.

Because here is a wild and gorgeous secret that can beautify even the weariest, most mundane of days: **God receives our offerings as so dearly precious.** As—like the woman's alabaster flask—a priceless perfume. What we offer up to him in love, no matter how trivial or menial it may seem, he receives with such a tender joy. Such a radiant delight.

Which means that **everything we do matters.** All our small moments that seem to go unseen. Unnoticed. Unsung. They are not lost to him. But, rather, glow like the candles that irradiate his smiling face.

And so may we offer them up: all the chores and sleepless nights, all the trivialities and monotony—*all* the moments of our ordinary lives. And may we see them reach God's tender gaze and light up his eyes with delight. A sight that can fill our weary days with wonder and turn our work into praise, as we see him *seeing us*, and ourselves held in the unbroken witness of his ever-loving gaze.

Crown Jewels

By Carolyn Etzel Branch

Beauty lived in the top right drawer of my mother's dresser and I could visit when I was good. On the left side, gleaming silver earrings and puddles of necklaces filled the dips of plastic egg crates. On the right, soft velvet boxes cradled jewels collected from all over the world. I opened the boxes with a muted snap, traced the contours of pendants, and then rummaged for more.

I plumbed the depths of beauty while my mother folded laundry behind me on the bed. If I stood on tiptoes, I could reach the back of the drawer and coax out strings of pearls and long silk scarves. Kneeling before the dresser, I learned the language of beautiful things: alabaster, amethyst, peridot, bronze. I adorned my vocabulary with princess cuts, chokers, and clasps. Best of all were the pairs of earrings, the longer and more intricate the better. My ears were not pierced yet and I felt this injustice keenly.

In memory now, certain characters from the drawer stand as beacons of my blossoming imagination. An amber teardrop pendant, the length of my small palm, taught me the meanings of "resin" and "petrified", and promptly became enchanted dryad jewelry. I remember a certain pair of silver coin earrings; I determined privately they were not from a department store but rather the Roman Empire. Nor could I be dissuaded that the pearl necklace with the tiny diamond clasp was not an antique from China, no matter what my mother said.

When she opened the drawer, it brimmed not with jewelry or accessories but with the years she lived in Prague. Where I saw legends, my mother saw time. Beauty's drawer divulged my father's tradition of bringing her back scarves from each of his travels and revealed long friendships which accumulated gifts. I nodded, listening to her memories while prodding a sharp earring back against the soft pad of my thumb.

"And what about these?" I asked, knowing all about them already. My mother leaned over me and saw the drawer housing the marriages of my grandmother and great-grandmother. I picked up my grandmother's engagement ring first, too big for my finger. Four prongs clutched the center diamond; tiny horizontal marquise diamonds scrolled outwards from its heart. Those same marquise stones embellished the gold wedding band. The rings lived in the drawer now, a testament to a wife turned widow only six months after the wedding. In just two decades, I'd slide a different marquise diamond set in a yellow gold band onto my finger, and that one would fit.

If I foraged, I could find my present family too. My mother taught me our family's birthstones—sapphire for one of my brothers, dawn-painted opal for her. I was disgruntled to discover that neither my birth month flower—carnation—nor its stone—garnet—were very precious, until I learned about the rarer form of garnets called "star garnets", which display a twinkling asterism when the light hits just right. Star garnets remythologized my sense of identity in the dresser drawer, and I would gleefully recognize them among the finery, a red so deep it looked black in shadow.

Every time I opened it, the drawer seemed to hold some new treasure to exult over. I never exhausted its contents. On a good day, I could convince my mother to let me pilfer treasures from the drawer rather than simply examine them. I'd end my visit to beauty with a turquoise bracelet looping one wrist and a fistful of jade. When the drawer closed I was bedecked in my mother's life, now inherited.

Sometimes lessons accompanied the visit; my mother attempted to cultivate not only admiration but care. Her hands which charmed piano keys at night after I went to bed also excelled at the meditation of untangling necklaces. She'd try to teach me the slow extricating of chains as a labor of contemplative satisfaction and not as a nuisance. "Always clip a necklace back together before storing it," she taught. "Otherwise it is much easier to get tangled."

I sighed loudly.

But the depiction of heaven's city in Revelation 21 read like a letter from an old friend. I could pick out the exact right crayon colors for twelve steps of precious stones. Pearl gates and a sea of glass called to me from the top dresser drawer. I knew exactly what a city of gold looked like.

***

Tarnished by age and tamed by a healthy distaste for the silence of God, these days I catch myself praying very politely. I budget out my requests in an attempt not to be disappointed. I prioritize in an effort to be better heard. Because I don't wish to overwhelm God, I pray like this: *I don't need all the beauty and blessings; I'm so content that I don't need all your favor, only one small thing. Won't you like me more if I take less from you?*

There are numerous ways to discover that the kingdom of heaven belongs to children, but the one that comes alive when confronted with beauty is the realization that when we become like children we recover an audacious hunger for wonder and good things. Children have not yet discovered the limitations of their guardians, and thus it is easy to understand that God has none. There is no back to the dresser drawer. If I pray like a child, I find myself with open hands before the throne. I pray like this: *I cannot fit all your glories on my wrists; you must delight in giving us beautiful things. Did you see, God? Did you see how beautiful that was? Bless me, Lord, in silk scarves and cool golden chains. I will curl sticky fingers around your halo set promises and shimmering presence. Let me wrap your love around my shoulders like a mother's benediction.*

The Giver loves to listen, so I can ask freely, knowing the quantity of my requests acknowledges the reality of my dependence. A hunger for blessing need not compete with contentment. I may hear, "No, you can't play in the dresser drawer right now." But I do not question whether the drawer exists, or whether I will someday have unrestrained access to its bounty. After all, no excess of blessing exists in the kingdom of heaven. In the kingdom of heaven, we are all decked out in inherited finery.

"Those who conquer will inherit these things, and I will be their God and they will be my children."
Revelation 21:7 NRSV

The Wonder of a Child

By Gina Gallagher

Have you ever watched a baby interact with the world? Everything is new and exciting. Every sound is fresh. Every experience is untried. A baby comes into the world totally dependent. Within one year's time, crawling becomes walking and babbling becomes talking. Within one year, a cup has been mastered and food is eaten with their own hand. The personality that God gave each child has come through loud and clear.

It is their childlike wonder that astounds me. Wonder that finds amazement in everything from their own toes to the human face before them. A small child has an infectious laugh. It is a belly laugh that catches the parent off guard, yet is the most delightful sound there is. The tearing of a piece of paper can cause uproarious laughter. Playing peek-a-boo can keep them entertained for quite some time. The world is new and undiscovered. One look into the eyes of a small child and you will see.

When does their sense of wonder go away? When does their uproarious laughter give way to a more subdued response? When does each new day become routine? When do they leave childhood for the more grown up world? It is not until we are adults that we long for the childlike wonder that was once ours. It is not until we are parents ourselves that we want to stop the clock from running so fast. I understand why J. M. Barrie felt the need to write *Peter Pan*. Barrie knew that the ticking clock comes for us all.

People would argue that childhood wonder must be left behind to make way for adulthood. We are in a rush to move to the next stage as quickly as possible. We tend to leave one stage behind, lock it in a box, and store it away somewhere. We fail to realize that keeping those stages close by will make us more compassionate.

I watched a child in a restaurant. Respectable manners should be taught and expected. However, a child is not a mini adult. Milk will spill, the fork will fall on the floor, and the people at nearby tables are interesting playmates. Food needs to be cut in bite sized pieces. Sitting still for the duration of the meal is quite difficult. Spoons sound like drums when they are played on the table. Salt and pepper shakers are interesting toys with which to play. I saw the frustration in the mother's eyes as she tried to have a nice lunch out. I saw the frustration in the child as he found every new sight and sound terribly interesting. There were warnings, pleadings, cajoling, and annoyance. Gone was the sense of wonder, newness, and excitement; in its place propriety ruled the day.

While waiting for an appointment, two little boys caught my eye. Just as I noticed them, they noticed me. The older brother was pretending to be a superhero. He stopped in front of me to make sure I took notice. In his mind, he wore a cape that he wrapped around him. In his imagination, his shoes were lightning fast. He pretended that his arm had the capability to do superhuman things. He loved that he had an audience.

His little brother was playing with a balloon. The string on the balloon intrigued him. He tried to keep the balloon on his lap but the balloon would not cooperate. Watching him learn about the world around him through a balloon was mesmerizing. The older brother would run around in circles and stop in front of me. He showed me his muscles and told me about his super strength. He ran in circles and told me about his fast shoes that can run and run and never stop. His mother looked at me and smiled; she has seen all this before.

I played along and entered into his world if only for a few minutes. His childlike wonder was captivating. Time seemed to stand still. The small world we inhabited for that short time took us to galaxies without leaving the chair. I know that his mother sees him play like this every day. I hope she realizes how very blessed she is. No store bought toy was anywhere nearby. It was not needed. A simple yellow balloon was enjoyed just as much, if not more, than the newest toy trend. The small boys poured themselves into their play and nothing more was needed. Every weapon used to fight the bad guys was at his disposal in his imagination. A battle was fought and won without leaving the room.

All grown-ups were once children... but only few of them remember it. (Antoine de Saint-Exupery, *The Little Prince*)

I want to remember it. I want to remember everything about it. I want to hear the sounds more clearly and see the sights more vibrantly. I want to fight the bad guys in the morning and fly to the moon at dusk. I want to see the world through the eyes of a child. I want to see the world with innocent eyes; eyes not jaded by life's experiences. It is possible. All we grown-ups need to do is remember.

I tell you the truth, anyone who will not receive the kingdom of God like a little child will never enter it. (Luke 18:17 NIV)

God appreciates childlike wonder. God holds up that wonder as an example of how we must enter the kingdom of God. We bring our adult selves to the table and think that is all the credentials we need. All of our accomplishments, awards, and success mean nothing if our heart is not childlike.

Grab hold of wonder. Catch a child's contagious laugh and belly laugh right along with him. Enter into a child's play and slay some dragons. Lay down the toys of your choosing and pick up your imagination. Become like a child. Be captivated by the world around you. See it for the wonder-filled world that it is. Spend a portion of each day remembering the child you once were. Cherish the memory.

Finding Grace in the Grass

By Bethany Peck

A round of robins flitted about the field, flying off into the trees as I approached them with my dogs crisscrossing around me. My cheeks dimpled with a soft grin as I took in the fresh hint of spring that was to come, while one lost robin still pecked around some dandelions for sustenance.

I see you Little Robin, making your way on your own. Now fly away and be free, I thought in kinship.

The recreation fields behind my home were most often empty, except for the robins, sparrows, and swallows, so I'd peruse the property, pretending I was the lady of an English manor out with my dogs for an afternoon stroll. On this day, as the earth was awakening from winter, my dogs wore their happy grins of freedom, ears flopping as they galloped in the spring breeze. Nearly identical, their dark, sleek bodies were flashes across the field— here a blue collar, there a red collar—a couple of primary colors chasing each other through the fresh green of grass overtaking the winter's umber palette.

Despite the unfurling of God's natural wonders, a quietness accompanied our walk, which was equally serene and unsettling. I thought Sundays would be different, but loss led me to a season of stillness, single with the hopes of motherhood only rich in my imagination. While the dogs ran about, visions of children scrambling over the distant playground and a blanket in the grass for a family picnic danced in my mind. Then, one of the dogs barked, disrupting my dreams and bringing me back to reality to find out what kind of mischief they'd found themselves in.

Most days did not go by without thanking God for my dogs, for the way they always supplied a source of joy in a time full of heartbreak. Some days, my pain stung like an angry yellow jacket queen, out in the April air again, alone and burdened with survival. On those days, I could have gone without even the hint of a smile were it not for my Pointer companions, who would do something silly, like wrestle over a stick, chase down a chickadee, or just lay their head on my lap. And, like a ray of sunshine all would feel warm and light again—even if only for a moment.

But one day, those rare smiles began to spring across my face more frequently, and not just from the dogs. My winter was thawing, and I could finally feel that bulbs buried deep in my heart might bloom again, just like that early feeling of spring when the robins appeared. My gratitude for survival guided me outdoors—day after day, week after week, month after month, season after season, year after year. The dogs always needed walking—no matter my mood—and my solitude always ached for the symphony of birdsong and the glowing light of day.

***

As we continued on our Sunday walk, with the robins watching us from the trees, I noticed the grass had gotten so high it would soon be time for the first mowing. Dandelions dotted the expanse; little orbs of sunshine soaked up the day's warmth, brightening my countenance. My heart felt the spring sun deeply too, as I breathed in the fresh scents that covered every inch of our make-believe manor.

The dogs slowed, and the sunshine seemed to beg me to rest, so I sat down in the damp grass. Always attuned to my senses and wanting to be near, the dogs came close to me and found themselves a good spot to lie down and scan the horizon—looking for more birds, surely. I eventually laid down too, grounding myself and welcoming a new perspective of the world. Individual blades of grass called my attention, and I admired the vibrancy of their color, contrasting the brown, dead patches underneath. The plethora of dandelions entranced me, their warm yellow color emanating a sense of peace, with each individual petal like a pillow beckoning me with comfort.

The solitude and simple beauty filled me with gratitude. These were not the Sundays I expected. And yet, they were abundantly good. Ache still existed within my heart, but wonder sparked by these simple delights soothed the sadness.

As I thought of the delicate beauty surrounding me, I also couldn't help but ponder the dandelion's transitory life. I remembered God's Word: *"The grass withers and the flowers fall..."* (Isa. 40:8a NIV). And isn't that me, too? With this quiet life I've been given, aren't I also just a mist on the wind? Yes, my time on Earth is finite, and the control I thought I had was just a mirage. But I can still have hope because *"...the word of our God endures forever"* (Isa. 40:8b NIV). God's Word lasts eternally and so does the love and redemption that are rooted in him. His Word is spring and resurrection. My grief is the fallow winter field—sowed by the Master Gardener—ready to burst forth with life again.

***

I fell in love with the grass that spring. The continued slowness of life allowed me to notice every awakening week. After the dandelions came the wild violets, then the buttercups, then the clover, then the dandelions seeding–even more whimsical as they whisked away in the wind. The violets became a favorite, as I visualized myself as a little girl sitting on the same hillside by our field, twirling them in my fingers, creating a little bouquet to delight my childhood self. I began to gather them again, a gift of love to the younger me–an offering of gratitude to my Father who's setting me free.

It's been years now since that walk in the field with both dogs, the robins, and my discovery of the dandelions. Sunday afternoons are still mostly quiet, and I think about what it would be like to watch my children grow as I instead notice the blooming of nature. But my heart has found so much joy in these simple wildflowers. Spring and the daily walks in my field provide great expectation. There is always a new week to look forward to when you're waiting for dandelions, buttercups, and violets. Their delight will lift my heart if it's hurting. The wonder of their beauty will not disappoint. Their fragility will point me to the One I can always trust.

I've since learned how hardy dandelions are, able to grow in less than ideal conditions, and I guess that's what I've been doing, too. I still wonder why my life has unfolded as it did, so I keep finding grace in the dandelions. And even though this present season is not blooming the cultivated roses I always imagined it would, there are wildflowers and herbs that give life and delight blooming here in their place. And what others think is a mere weed may just be the greatest beauty to a soul who needs reviving—for this natural wonder is a true beauty in the eyes of her Beholder.

***

A man who also suffered with deep sadness two and half centuries ago asked similar questions, yet grounded himself in trust. William Cowper's beautiful hymn, "God Moves in a Mysterious Way," which had tears flowing down my cheeks the first time I ever heard it in church a few years ago, concludes,

> *"God's purposes will ripen fast,*
> *Unfolding every hour.*
> *The bud may have a bitter taste,*
> *But sweet will be the flower.*
> *Blind unbelief is sure to err*
> *And scan his work in vain.*
> *God is his own interpreter,*
> *And he will make it plain."*[1]

One day, God will answer all our questions whispered in the deafeningly quiet moments. What grieves your heart will bloom with heavenly reward: *"The bud may have a bitter taste, But sweet will be the flower."* The grass will fade. Bodies will weaken, but the everlasting Springtime will overtake us with glorious beauty—with a *shalom* that wipes away our tears. God will meet you in the grass. Let him lie you down in green pastures, as the Good Shepherd who guides you where you need to be.

---

1 William Cowper, God Moves in a Mysterious Way, 1774. https://hymnary.org/text/god_moves_in_a_mysterious_way

For now, as I await this year's flowering grass, I will dream about the robins, walk through the fields, and bask in the warmth of bright days. And as I go out to walk among the wildflowers, I know my Good Shepherd will welcome me to rest in his wonder. Then one glorious day, I'll be free and see how *sweet will be the flower.*

Brush with Sublime

By Kristine Amundrud

Soft glow of neon lights hummed against the night air as I pulled into the petrol station. Luminous pillars from light reflecting off ice crystals, set the stage for a celestial scene. I lost myself in the rare optical illusion before being jolted back to reality—a feeling of homesickness. Dim realization had dawned and as fear flickered near closing time, an internal filament burned out. Empty gas tank, a wallet left at home—divine enters in through minor inconvenience.

Praying for solutions feels like putting God in a box. *Can the creator of the universe override our reluctant flesh?* Far from practical, refreshingly radical, he does all according to his will.

Before panic ensued, out of thin hushed air, a stranger swooped in, as if to utter: *do not be afraid.* Warm words led into another realm. *"I'd be happy to put twenty dollars worth in your tank,"* he said. A rusted old sedan sat parked outside. I hadn't heard it approaching—ramshackle jalopy, yet there was money to spare?

So ordinary. He had dark hair parted to the side and wore a worn navy jacket. He spoke: *"My name is Dan–happy to help–pay-it-forward if you can. Oh, and would you pray for my wife with cancer?"* Not your typical gas-station conversation, I agreed to pray without hesitation. Stepping outside, I caught a glimpse of his wife in the passenger seat. Blond curls framed her pale face.

Breath condensed into a cloud while I pondered the encounter. A click of the gas nozzle woke me from my reverie, and I felt an impulse to pray together. Turning to run back towards him, I found that angels seldom linger. Departing silently into nothingness, I had missed my opportunity. The briefest encounter had been my brush with sublime. Incontestably holy. Entertained by an angel with no forwarding address, I was initially unawares. Hospitality supernaturally granted to me. I was a guest, when

Dan ought to have been mine. Be that all as it may. I pray for them to this day.

> *Do not neglect to show hospitality to strangers, for*
> *thereby some have entertained angels unawares.*
> *(Hebrews 13:2 ESV)*

Seeds of Wonder

By Cyndy Chisare

In the lushness of spring, after the fear of frost has passed and the trees are budding and blossoming, I begin to look forward to planting an herb garden. I count the days until my hands can be immersed into the cool, winter-moist soil, searching with fingers to unearth those abandoned acorns, earthworms and remembering how satisfying it feels to have my hands in dirt again.

It's not a huge garden by anyone's standard, but it's my garden; full of rosemary and thyme, lavender, oregano and basil. Jostling and elbowing for space and light, my herbs thrive happily in the garden in a harmony of fragrances warmed by the sun. Within weeks, oregano, basil and thyme will be chosen to add their flavors to an all-day tomato sauce, gently simmering on the stove; and thyme sprigs will add just the right subtleness to a chicken that has been golden-roasted in lemon and garlic. Intoxicating aromas, both inside and out, that linger long after the last of the sauce has been mopped up with crusty bread and pots have been washed.

Into my small Eden-like paradise, I add a "fairy-sized" house on a bed of moss, and small bee hives and birdhouses are scattered throughout. Moon snails from the depths of the ocean and sun-bleached seashells become a footpath between the thyme. These are created for my own "little people" —my grandchildren—who will peer into the garden and pretend to live among the fragrance and tumble of herbs and the buzzing of bees. They find absolute delight in my Eden, looking for any tell-tale signs of any resident or the night magic left behind, like the remains of a hatched robin's egg that mirrors the color of a summer's sky.

Fragrant herbs, seashells and a tiny home are the things that can be seen and felt and tasted in the garden; but into this garden, I also sow old-fashioned seeds of orange nasturtiums, pink, blue and salmon-hued sweet peas. These are the seeds that I have cho-sen for me, for their romance, their nostalgic charm; but mostly for their fragrance.

They have become my seeds of wonder; of long-ago vacations at the most enchanting of places—the home of my grandparents. They are the seeds that remind me of blue, cloudless skies, cooling off in the river and children's games at twilight. They are the seeds of the fragrance of a summer afternoon on a sweet-pea-trellised porch.

Our once-a-year vacations to visit our grandparents were al-ways an event to be anticipated. As soon as school was out, my sister and I would pack pajamas and toothbrushes; bathing suits and dolls, eagerly waiting for a week of adventure, of discovery and all things extraordinary.

There were cousins with which to play hide-and-seek in the hydrangea bushes, a grape arbor to raid for its sweet, purpled fruit, and adults to annoy when the ice cream truck turned onto the street. Big, sun-ripened blackberries grew wild in the alley-ways, waiting to be picked by small, juice-stained fingers for cobblers. At twilight, as the sky turned all pink and purple, just as the evening became quiet, there were thousands of fireflies to catch in mason jars.

In the cool of early morning, the never-ending chores of garden-tending would begin. There were green beans to pick, to wash and then snap for dinner. The tomatoes needed to be re-staked and checked for theft from marauding blue jays and crows; and of course, peas needed to be shucked and plants wa-tered and weeded. Our chores in the garden were rewarded with hard-earned quarters that were immediately spent at the local grocery and penny-candy store, a garden of childhood delights!

Heat-hazy, mid-afternoons were time to ourselves. We would take turns on the tire swing in the shade of the old elm, drinking Kool-aid and eating peanut butter and jelly sandwiches, always discussing life as only 8-year-olds understood; watching out for snakes in the garden, hoping to go swimming in the river, and looking for the kittens in the garage. Everyday moments of sum-mer life that engraved memories and hatched dreams, while we dutifully watched my grandfather's corn grow and ripen in their husks under the sun.

But even in the middle of our wonder-filled vacation, there was that one dreaded chore that no one ever volunteered for, the one that required the bravest of brave hearts to negotiate an obstacle course rife with land mines—that was navigating a path to the hen house to gather eggs for breakfast. This early-morning reconnoiter risked an all-out assault from the resident rooster, a ginormous Rhode Island Red, as mean as any junkyard dog and twice as fast, with talons so sharp any injury would surely result in certain death. It required childhood stealth, and a knowing when to wait and when to run without receiving any deadly fire to life or limb.

Toward the end of the day's work, as the sun slid toward the horizon, parents, grandparents, uncles, aunts and the occasional neighbor all began to congregate in the shade and coolness of the front porch. The sound of the old rockers keeping time to the intensity of the gossip and porch stories being told. There were cold drinks and the much loved aroma of my grandfather's cherry, pipe tobacco mingled with the sun-wilted sweet peas.

Whatever the occasion and whoever was present on that trellised porch, invitations would always be extended for "a bite to eat," to share with the family in dinner conversation, laughter and prayer. After dinner, everyone would return to the early-evening cool of the porch for freshly made cobbler, for a pipe, and even more gossip before the deep purples and shadows of twilight settled over everything.

Those blissful summer days—a trellised porch fragrant with sweet peas, alleyways overgrown with blackberries and fireflies at twilight—have become somewhat dimmed with the passage of time. But at the foundation of those days was a home whose welcome never ended. A home whose very foundation was built upon grace received through faith and summers that were filled with every unimaginable wonder to a child learning to map their way in the world. A child who learned that everyday kindnesses were extended to everyone, and every single day could bring endless possibilities.

When I think about those long-ago days, I realize that, yes,
I might be trying to recreate those memories, not from a child's
perspective, but from the perspective of being a grandmother; of
hearing my own grandchildren's laughter, watching the bubbles
they blow floating off into the air. They are growing up in a time
much different from the one I inhabited at their age. A time that
seems more riddled with dangers; but it is my hope that they will
continue to find a bit of wonder and light in my home and garden, much as I did with my grandparents.

The good times and the not-so-good ones, the skinned knees,
being chased by the Rhode Island Red, and whole quarters to
spend at the candy store, were fundamental stuff of childhood;
but I can't imagine one single thing that I would ever change.
That old, wooden-trellised front porch that was witness to many
conversations and prayer allowed me to feel the humming and
the vibration of childhood in my veins. It was a place and a time
that had the wonder of everyday life worn into its floorboards;
and that wonder was deeply written onto my own heart.

The Toy Subject

By Cheryl Eichman

"What is your favorite childhood toy?" I am not sure why I started asking this get to know you question, but I am glad I did. Before answering, the responder's eyes glimmer. I watch as the individual digs through their memories until a single toy, worn smooth from years of love, is retrieved and shared. The responses vary from cars to crayons, swings to sewing kits. Even mud has made the list.

This question, while fun, reveals something deeper. Barring childhood trauma, everyone once had a spirit of wonder, and for most, there was also a point where it went quiet. Most don't acknowledge this directly, but after the toy subject comes to a close, the smile changes and the eyes lose their magic. Facial expressions turn serious as they pack up and store the toy memory to make room for the "real" discussions. No longer is the speaker a 3-year-old willing to stare at every stranger passing by. Mud between toes fades away into stilettos. The 10-year-old rides away on his red bike to be replaced by a man in a red tie.

We move back into the put-together, serious versions of ourselves, out of respect for whatever topic we are discussing. This isn't a bad thing per se, but there is a loss of magic. The childhood confidence leaves as quick as it came. Life gets heavier, words hold less whimsy. The shift between child and adult persona is tangible. My daughter saw this dichotomy at an early age. At four years old, I found her in her room processing this. She looked up at me through crocodile tears and sobbed, "Mommy, I don't want to grow up." My first instinct was to reply, "Me either pumpkin, me either."

So often "grown-up" means we lose our joy, our wonder and our play. It means we get old in our soul, not just our bodies. We believe that we are incapable of learning new things, that we must master our crafts, and that our schedules must be completely full. There is very little room for inquisitiveness, very little room for mistakes, and very little room for freedom. We forget that along with responsibility, respect, and wisdom, adulthood also must include wonder and fun. A critical piece of a well-functioning adult is joy. Grown-up doesn't mean we cannot play and dream, it just means we have to discern when it is appropriate.

Knowing how worried my daughter was about growing up, we planned her "rights of passage" trip accordingly. We did a trip for each of our children at 12. We planned these trips with the specific purpose of ushering our kids into young adulthood. My daughter's trip was time at an amusement park in Florida. This was a sacrifice of time and money, but it was important that she started out her young adult adventure engaging with fun. During her trip we rode roller coasters, ate themed treats, got drenched on water rides, and screamed our voices horse. Our imaginations came to life from beloved movies and shows depicted on the rides. Even though our ages spanned 30 years, all of us felt the wonder of play.

To be honest, while we planned the trip for my daughter, it ended up being important to all of us. With the heaviness that comes with my husband's counseling practice and my people-intense job, we were forgetting how to play. Even my son, just two years older than my daughter, was morphing into staidness, just as my daughter feared for her future self. The passions in our lives were becoming chores, the rhythms of our lives were becoming routines. This rights of passage trip for our daughter to step into adulthood also became a rights of passage trip for the rest of us to step back into childlike wonder.

Somehow we forget that life doesn't stop at 25. We can still grow, learn, and live at 26. Wonder, laughter, and adventure are still an option in your 40s and 50s. The magic does not need to stop once our brains are fully developed. This shouldn't be hard for me to remember since my 80-year-old mother still instigates water fights at family reunions. Youth shimmers in her eye as she hands a water balloon to one of my cousins. She then steps inside laughing while everyone else attains sopping clothes and water-wrinkled feet.

People often perceive the behaviors associated with wonder as trite, immature, dramatic, or even wasteful. These connotations persuade "responsible adults" to avoid it. When we work so hard for respect, we don't want to lose it by being whimsical. But contrary to this popular presumption, when done in an appropriate space, wonder doesn't spotlight immaturity, it spotlights joy. It doesn't bring about ignorance, it brings about humility. Play literally brings our brains out of darkness as neurons light up within our brain. Wonder ushers us into the space occupied by amazement and imagination—two words that share a room with their sister, faith. This is a place where greatness occurs.

Wonderment and unpretentiousness bring us back into the behavior of our salvation. Analytics, flow-charts, data points, schedules, these things don't bring us to Christ's feet with the childlike posture he asks for. These things invite him into a boardroom while he is inviting us to a playground. We ask for a business meeting and he is asking for a picnic.

So how do we learn to be in wonder again? It does not require an expensive trip or roller coasters. Thankfully, it is more accessible than that, though not necessarily easier. Wonder requires space. We need space from schedule and rote thinking. We need space from concern, striving, and perfecting. Separating from these familiar voices is necessary, despite the discomfort and insecurity it may cause. Put perfecting and striving in timeout for an hour and don't sit in the hallway waiting for them. Step out the door into fresh air, see where you go without them.

Wonder asks us to let go of expectations and apprehension. It asks you to go forth even if you don't understand. That is part of why it is magical. It is unhindered. And if it still feels awkward, ask a friend for help. Invite them to laugh with you, imagine with you, exhale with you. And if you still don't know where to start, maybe ask them what their favorite childhood toy was.

Wonderstruck

Reflections on a Meteor Shower Watch Party

by Bailey Gillespie

August 2015

The sky is full of stars. And I am ready to be wonderstruck.

I've seen many shooting stars before but never stayed awake long enough to witness this phenomenon the night sky has to offer for those who *wait*. Tonight's the night. But I don't want to experience it alone, so I made a private Facebook event and invited my community to a virtual watch party. Ten... 20... 30... The RSVPs send a thrill to my fingertips. I set an alarm on my phone, just in case I fall asleep.

Tonight, 37 friends from around the country willingly give up their sleep, anticipating the most highly publicized event of the summer: the Perseid Meteor Shower.

It's almost midnight, but the air is still humid. I sink my muscles into the earth, sprawled on a fiesta blanket the color of sunsets or swirled sherbet. A breeze lifts the redwood boughs, silhouetted against a sky pricked with constellations. Moisture seeps from pockets of muddy grass as I lay on my back, arms folded under my head. Alone, at peace, I watch the blackness stretch west and smile as Coldplay plays from my phone.

Each summer, the Perseids peak in mid-August when Earth interacts with debris left in our atmosphere from the comet 109P/Swift-Tuttle. It's known for being the best meteor shower of the year, reaching 50-100 meteors per hour, depending on region and light pollution (NASA.org). Tonight, they culminate at midnight, Pacific Standard Time, here in Northern California. I'm excited to get real-time check-ins from people in other time zones experiencing the show before me. I imagine this is a little what time traveling feels like.

Snacks, I think. *There should be snacks. And music!*

I can already imagine the playlist: "Cassiopeia" by Sara Bareilles, "A Sky Full of Stars" by Coldplay, the WALL-E film score, anything by Explosions in the Sky or Sleeping at Last, and, of course, "Meteor Shower" by Owl City.

I lay now and wait, my eyes attuned and my heart expectant. Music streams from my portable speaker as our playlist (hand-crafted for an optimum star-viewing experience) plays songs bursting with whimsy. The park is abandoned. Behind me, a swingset creaks ever-so-gently in the breeze, lit up by two flood lamps. First comes a plane. Then a satellite. I don't see any comets. But wait!—bats! Yes, it's a cauldron of bats, flapping their scalloped wings.

It's a beautiful night, but I wonder: will they ever come? These stars, this other-ness I long to see? Or was this just misplaced hope?

****

After an hour of silence, the wait is over. I stop worrying. I stop thinking.

I am spellbound by wonder.

Six meteors cascade across the sky, and I witness the most resplendent shooting star in my history as a star-gazer.

"Team North Star reporting," writes my friend Kristen in Owatonna, Minnesota. "We have some high-altitude clouds here, but we're still heading out!" She posts a photograph of a red-and-white striped *serape* blanket and an assortment of on-theme party snacks: a bag of Boom Chicka Pop, bottles of blackberry-ginger soda, and Milky Way Midnight minis.

Kristen understood the assignment. She posts a second update: "We drove out to an old one-room schoolhouse and laid our blankets at the edge of a cornfield. The Milky Way was spectacular, and several meteors shot right across it."

"What direction am I supposed to look for this meteor shower?" writes another friend. "I've seen one owl, four planes, and about five mosquitoes."

"We went up to Wisconsin to get away from city lights, armed with wine, chips, guacamole, hummus, and vegetables. Such a great little road trip."

I'm sleepy. Also cold. I pull my socks higher and swaddle myself in a throw blanket, wishing I'd brought a thermos of herbal tea. The dew from the grass soaks through the *serape*, dampening my legs, but I can't quit now. I can't let my friends down. I keep thinking there's a stranger behind me, but it's just the old swingset creaking away.

Facebook comments continue to pour in. Some friends share their joy, others their longing. Both are sacred.

"Didn't see anything here in western Kentucky, but it is a beautiful night!" writes an older woman who lives alone. "Thinking of all of you stargazers."

"This was my eight-year-old son's first meteor shower," shares Peter, a dad of two. "He and my daughter headed out back with me at 2:00 AM, whereupon I threw a few sleeping bags down on the concrete for padding and commenced Perseidfest 2015."

The last post gives me an ache:

> "I'm reminded of the last time I was on this same broodingly dark street looking for streams of light. It was last summer, attempting to watch the same group of meteors on an overcast night with the woman I thought I would marry. But tonight, I was alone, looking for signs of movement in the sky as possible signs that life could move forward. Even the stars don't remain in one place forever as they shoot from one existence to another. Praying a little prayer, I was thankful for the beauty God showed me as the Perseids fell to the earth, even though my heart has felt like beauty departed."

* * *

In earlier times, astronomers, farmers, sailors, scientists, wise men, and poets depended on stars for their livelihood and navigation. But in the 21st century, so few of us take the time to turn our gaze upward. Tonight, we push against the routine in search of something greater. We exchange sleep and routine for adventure, mystery, beauty, and wonder (all the time wondering if the journalists are correct: will it be the cosmic event of the year?).

Tonight, we worship outside church walls, feeling our finitude as dewy toes and soda bottles contrast against the celestial tapestry.

As enchanting as this night is, it's not the Perseids that captivate me. It's the 37 people who carved out two hours of their lives in the middle of the night to spend time with friends and family, eager and expectant. In an age where you can't make people RSVP more than 24 hours in advance to just about anything, this is no small miracle. This is what I will remember for the rest of my life.

The timing of this experience is also not lost on me. One month later, I will lose my job at the local university, not a mile away, when a financial crisis hits.

I once heard someone compare spiritual darkness (the dark night of the soul) to a womb where new life germinates. This womb is a nurturing, holding space like the belly of the earth where seeds are planted. **These metaphors of darkness remind us there is always more happening than we can see.** Perhaps this darkness tonight is holding me, preparing me for a greater darkness to come. It is a darkness more all-consuming than I have ever known, leading to a series of griefs from the accumulation of losses: a beloved job, my apartment, my academic community, and my tuition waived for a graduate degree. An utter and complete stripping.

Yet I believe there is always more happening than we can see. God's Spirit is in all things and goes before us, behind us, above us, and below us, hemming us in, preparing us for what's ahead. Beyond even that looming sorrow is a time of restoration for me—a new job, a new degree, and a wider community given back tenfold like Job's story in the Old Testament. This cycle will keep repeating as life marches on. **I am certain, somewhere deep down, this meteor shower is forming in me a belief that beauty always unfolds right there alongside the darkness.**

***

From the fields of Kentucky to the suburbs of California, God meets each of us in 37 different ways. Here, right where we're at.

The paradox of life: light and darkness, glory and grief, love and longing, wildness and routine, God's nearness and his vastness.

My eyelids grow heavy. The playlist ends, and I can no longer feel my feet. I lift my body from the soaked blanket and brush crumbs from my shirt. Leaving the park, I glance up once more, wonderstruck.

Mission accomplished.

Perseid Viewing Party Starter Kit
- Snacks (popcorn, fruit, chocolate, drinks)
- Phone
- Bluetooth speaker
- Picnic blanket
- Extra blanket for warmth
- Waterproof pants or padding
- A fellow kindred
- Optional: A star-tracker app like Night Sky

When Wonder Sings

By Caitlin Lore

The first time I heard a woodpecker on my neighborhood walk, I spent ten minutes searching the tree line for him. It wasn't until I shifted my gaze and felt a cramp in my neck that I gave up my quest.

The neighborhood was quiet, but then again it was seven am on a summer morning, and his drumming on the bark echoed down the block. I stood on my favorite corner between the widow's and the artist's house, as I'd so named them for their architecture, but he was impossible to find in all of the foliage.

I spent many mornings that summer searching for him, but just as I'd catch a flicker of movement, he would hobble around the tree and disappear.

That season, my own faith quieted, too.

***

By winter, my grief consumed me as I wandered the neighborhood, my daily walks a desperate need in the darkness. The trees were empty, as felt my soul, after my most recent round of hormone testing.

Out of range. Out of range. Out of range.

I was barely 37 and yet my ovaries were failing.

The snow crunched under my feet as I placed one foot in front of the other, my walk the same every day because wandering felt wrong. Stay on the path. Just keep trying.

Round and round went the cycles, went my walks, went my faith.

Drum-drum-drum-drum-drum-drum-drum went the woodpecker.

The moment I looked up, I spotted his red cap bobbing on the enormous trunk of the dead oak tree. A *red-bellied*, I thought as the starkness of the red against the muted winter caught me off guard; the tiny bird happily hopping around looking for food. He paused, drumming again at nineteen beats a second, before flying off across the street.

Without even trying, I had found him.

In that moment, I realized he had most likely been there all along, a spot of wonder flitting around the dying trees.

***

The red-bellied woodpecker is one of the world's most easily recognizable woodpeckers. Even though they have a slightly red belly, it fades over time; thus, they are more known for the red cap the males sport. They are often a solitary creature, except during mating season spanning late winter through early spring.

That winter elapsed slowly, filled with more tests.

We could try again, I told my husband. *Another cycle. It's possible.*

We rested. I walked. Though my odds of finding my woodpecker in the afternoons were slim, I trudged out through snow and wind chills just for a glimpse of his red cap. I counted the times I saw him, few and far between as winter gave way to darkness.

We counted days. We tried again. I looked for my friend.

Spring nearly arrived. We were ready, but my eggs weren't.

***

Weeks later, our city cut down his tree.

Two steps around the artist's corner and another tree felled. My tears came silently as the last of my wonder disappeared.

Too much loss, I whispered to myself. *Not you too.*

Yet I kept walking—through the pain, and the grief, and the season.

I started looking up more, noticing the flutters and the songs.

There was a downy, at Tom's house, flitting about the aged tree.

A charm of finches outside my own back window, lined up on the fence as if waiting for their school lesson.

The shocking blue of a jay in the church parking lot, a new faith tradition grounding me.

And there—soaring high over the park—a bald eagle. Something I never imagined I'd witness in my lifetime.

Despite the loss of my hopes and a future imagined, I wondered what it would be to soar.

***

It didn't take me long to pick up his call this winter, a shrill *kwirr, kwirr, kwirr* that echoed down the road as I walked out of my grief.

Even if I couldn't see him, he was there.

I must have stood on the corner at least ten minutes searching the trees, waiting for him to appear.

Just as I turned the corner, they started to sing.

I looked back, spotting one red cap and another slightly faded dancing around the withered bark.

A back and forth song bursting of life.

So I turned toward home, my own faith less quiet.

He had been there all along simply waiting for her to find him.

Milk Glass Memories

By Calli Shea Birch

I cradle the delicate milk glass, turning it toward the light to inspect the hand-painted cherry blossoms decorating its sides. My earliest memories rush back to me in fragments, like faded snapshots in a vintage photo album, each one connected to my senses.

June in East Texas, and I'm surrounded by abundance. Plump blackberries, ripened on the vine, stain my fingers, lips, cheeks— their purple sugars overwhelming my tastebuds. Not afraid of the occasional thorn, my fingers navigate the maze of climbing tendrils and gather a tiny harvest into the apron that drapes from my frame. Maybe, just maybe, I'll pick enough berries for Mama Bowlin's homemade cobbler.

An aromatic fragrance and an old man's mumbling call me from the garden fence to the fig tree. Pausing to deposit my berry bounty into a small basket, I lick each finger clean and wipe my hands along the apron front. My great-grandfather stoops below broad leaves, his pipe smoke intermingling with the honeyed sweetness of tender figs. He carefully hoists me upon the bottom branch and stays close to the tree as I climb.

My hands grasp each sturdy limb, pulling me up higher—further up and further in—until I've almost reached the top of the fig tree, its thick foliage shading me from the summer sun. A wide bough serves as a seat, cradling me as I begin to pluck the bell-shaped fruit. Again my apron proves handy, forming a little pouch to collect the figs that will later create my favorite jam.

Looking back, I now consider my three-year-old self. Long before I knew of King Solomon, I somehow perceived the ancient symbol of peace and blessing during his reign, when the people "lived in safety, everyone under their own vine and under their own fig tree." If you had asked me where I felt abundant love as a young child, I would have told you: Mama and Papa Bowlin's garden. Retired teachers living modestly, they built my earliest childhood memories while my young parents worked hard to build me a future. Yet, a product of their time, my great-grandparents never said the words, silently showing love in a thousand ways while simply replying "same here" to every "I love you" I sang out.

They loved me with Shake 'N Bake chicken on a CorningWare plate and extra Red Hots in a glass candy dish. They loved me while I splashed in a metal wash tub or jumped into piles of leaves or hugged Papa's neck just to hear his melodious "ummmhmmm" response. Forming the foundation of my first memories, the absolute wonder of their simple, servant-hearted love.

My hands touch the small grooves of milk glass, teal forget-me-nots lining its scalloped rim and tiny pedestal feet arching elegantly underneath. Mama Bowlin served me egg custard in this dish, and to this day, I can still taste the lost recipe.

The Work of Wonder

By Emily Boulter

"I came here to study hard things—rock mountain and salt sea—and to temper my spirit on their edges. 'Teach me thy ways, O Lord' is, like all prayers, a rash one, and one I cannot but recommend." —Annie Dillard, Holy the Firm

I couldn't agree more with Annie. Mountains claimed my imagination, heart, and obsession long ago, and I doubt I will ever tire of their splendor, mystery, and indomitable wilderness. I doubt I will ever lose the sense of utter wonder that washes over me when I leave the symphony of city and man behind and embark into God's orchestration of nature, forest, rock, and weather. The deeper I go, the more deeply I understand the ways of my Savior.

Wonder, as defined by the Oxford dictionary is, "a feeling of surprise and pleasure that you have when you see or experience something beautiful, unusual or unexpected."

A synonym of this delightful word is *awe*.

I don't believe it is necessarily difficult to discover wonder in the natural world. Our Creator really outdid himself when he imagined and spoke into being the myriad displays of beauty, curiosity, and mystery we dwell within. Earth is a humble word for such a glorious canvas. And yet, the culture we find ourselves in seems to prefer the unraveling of beauty and the elevation of the carnal. We are constantly beckoned to *descend*.

To be honest, who can blame it? Without God, without hope, without purpose or identity...why wonder? Why ascend? Whereto?

"The hardest thing of all to see is what is really there." —J.A. Baker, The Peregrine

But I believe that as Christians we are called to be ambassadors of wonder, to explore, dwell, and cultivate what I believe is a fundamentally holy work. Wonder may be easy when surrounded by mountains, with grand vistas, or when the salted air of oceans tangles our hair and thrills our senses...but what about our everyday? What of when we are home, at work, caring for those whose wellbeing relies upon our every decision? Isn't wonder and the cultivation of imagination for those fickle moments of leisure, for weekends, and holidays?

Isn't seeking wonder—and the wonderful—a waste of our precious time?

As I study Scripture, creation, and explore my role as a created being by a creative God I keep running into this astonishing thought: what if we were actually created for wonder?

"Unlike the other gods
you are not satisfied with holocausts
and the sweet smell of smoke.
Unlike the other gods
you do not let us be
but come and pitch your tent
with ours and sniff out
all we do. You are not satisfied
to have us satisfied,
to leave well enough alone."
—Madeleine L'Engle, A Cry Like a Bell

Since the beginning of man, God called Adam into creative partnership with himself, to fill the world, subdue it, to name all creatures, and to worship. The chief end of man is to what? Glorify God and enjoy him forever.

To *glorify*. To *enjoy*. To marvel, wonder, explore, expound, delight, and dwell in awe of the beauty, love, mercy, and character of our God. How can we accomplish this if we are not actively looking for, cultivating, and instructing in the art, work, and posture of wonder? God is not satisfied with the rote, with actions and sacrifice void of meaning. He demands our hearts, our souls, our bodies, our minds, our devotion. *Our awe.*

"Many Christians spend their best effort on trying to be holy or on doing good deeds, and they forget to see." —Ben Palpant, Letters from the Mountain

We forget the premise of good works, the premise of our very faith. Can we fully embrace a faith in the sacrifice, redemption, and eternal victory of Jesus Christ without wonder? Without utter and complete awe and delight at this mysterious truth? Can we evangelize effectively without stewarding that first juncture of desperation, hope, and thrill of faith that brought us to our own knees before the throne of a King who would die to save us from our own rebellion?

Wonder, I'm finding...is *necessary*.

Just like any important work, sport, craft, or health regimen, the healthy imagination—the discipline of wonder—requires practice. It requires us to show up and pay attention. If we never go to class, we will never learn anything, much less be able to uphold the tradition and extend the wisdom gained to the next generation. What we behold in wonder isn't just for our own delight or our own expansion...it is for the glory of God, for the edification of his people; it is a spark that contains the potential to cause wildfire in the hearts and imaginations of others. In a sense...what we feed our imaginations and the context in which we exercise our wonder can shape culture, can contribute to the renewal and expansion of the world.

How stunning this is, that our Creator would grant to his created works the cultivation, stewardship, and enjoyment of beauty, goodness, and truth. What a wonder that he provides us with eternal inspiration, with overflowing reason, with never ending love. What a wonder that we get to belong to an anthem and epic of redemption, of re-creation as citizens of heaven itself.

Beauty, wonder, and imagination are often considered the prerogative of artists, poets, writers, and musicians. We often leave this aspect of culture and civilization to those deemed "gifted" at such things, those born with a tendency toward creativity. While beauty may be the primary duty of the artist, I believe it is also the work of every Christian.

"This is the irrational season
when love blooms bright and wild.
Had Mary been filled with reason

there'd have been no room for the child."
—*Madeleine L'Engle,* A Cry Like a Bell

Expanding our capacity for wonder expands our capacity to know God. Practicing a posture of worship, of hopeful delight, of informed bewilderment at who God is and his faithfulness towards us affords us glimpses of all that will be—of earth made new. In wonder we ready ourselves for the coming of Christ.

Wonder doesn't rely upon the obviously beautiful. Gratitude doesn't rely upon the largeness of the gift. Worship doesn't rely upon the enormity of the problem. We walk with Emmanuel... God With Us. *With us* in the mundanity of our everyday, in our waking and sleeping and sleeplessness, in our pain and doubt and disappointment. In our frailty. In our brokenness. Wonder doesn't always equate happiness. It is capable of holding so much more than the spectrum of positivity. It is the reality of Christ's strength in our weakness, of his perfect sacrifice when our efforts fall so very short, of eternal and promised victory as we experience so vividly the fallenness of this first, divided world.

"And do not be conformed to this world, but be transformed by the renewing of your mind, that you may prove what is that good and acceptable and perfect will of God." —Romans 12:2

Wonder...it builds our foundation and draws us back to the One in whom we have our very being.

The Kindness of Strangers

By Kenzie McGregor

I'm always amazed at the kindness of strangers, and know I shouldn't be. Some, perhaps, are angels, ministering spirits who've seen the face of God and lived to whisper grace. But all a gentle breath of wind on a humid August day, or a splash of rain to parched red clay. Like the older lady I met at Walmart last Sunday who let me cut in front of her in line. And then asked the newly-arrived man behind her if he wanted to cut too. He consented with feigned pushback. And I wondered how long she would stand in line, allowing strangers to bypass her grocery cart that wasn't all that full.

Or the lady from Nashville I met in Texas, a poet, who listened raptly to my first ever lecture-style presentation on Flannery O'Connor. A bright spot in my exhaustion and anxiety, my twenty-four-year-old-self lack of self worth. A new friend.

Or the visiting author, a brilliant mind, who willingly relinquished her head-of-the-table chair to an autistic teen who arrived late to her workshop. Without faltering she continued her lecture standing, making him feel wanted and appreciated—and us graced instead of ignored.

Or the woman who pointed out beverage options from an American Airlines's menu to the non-English speaking mother between us. A can of Sprite, she concurred. This same woman also picked up the two year-old daughter's soft pink blanket from the germy floor and helped the mother wrap the child. Or the flight attendant who didn't hesitate to help the mother and her grumpy, bed-headed daughter extract their luggage from the plane. Perhaps it was more than just a job for her.

This list continues in many ways, if we look around us. But that's often the problem. When I remember the small kindnesses I witness every day and forget, I wonder. I feel guilt and shame and a longing for something more. Because it turns out that beyond our screens and glass walls and text bubbles, we aren't just red or blue. Roe or Wade. Baptist or Catholic. We're more than American or American-hyphenated—we're human. And we experience what it means to be fragile and vulnerable and limited and emotional and flawed with others. To have hurts and to hold hurts until death. To feel, to love, to hope together.

This is grace, and I shouldn't be amazed that the hands of feet of Jesus should miraculously and mysteriously remain on earth to this day. That the same grace he showed to Thomas, to lepers, to a menstruating woman—to adulterers and tax collectors and children—should flower in my life today.

As I meditate on his kindness and see it reflected, however dimly, in others, I wish for a greater kindness to light in myself. And pray that maybe one day, I too can be any kind of vessel for grace.

The Wonder of Peace Amid Waves

By Bethany Valyou

Moving my dinner around my plate, I let out a soft sigh and met the gaze of my husband sitting across the table. His eyes reflected the same exhaustion and sadness I knew people saw when they looked at my face. I smiled a half-convincing *"see, we're getting through this"* smile—a smile he returned with the same look of helpless defeat.

It had only been a couple of weeks since we'd lost our baby during a heartbreaking miscarriage—our second loss in less than six months. And while the arms of our family and church community held us tight, and God's faithful presence remained undeniably steadfast, we found ourselves in a state of paralyzing numbness, unsure of how to move forward.

Breaking his gaze, my husband's eyes suddenly darted to something moving past the bay window beside my chair.

"Is that a cat?" he pointed to a small dark figure slinking through the bushes.

We were used to seeing skunks, raccoons, and even crows the size of cats in our yard, but never before had we seen a cat on our property, aside from the two that lived in our home. And with the exception of our next-door neighbor, we didn't exactly live in close quarters with any neighboring houses.

Upon closer examination through the glass, the meandering animal in our yard was, indeed, a small cat—a thin, hungry-looking tabby who seemed to have just appeared out of the woods behind our house. My husband and I looked at each other and, without speaking a single word, agreed to do all we could to take care of this cat until we could find his owner.

It was, after all, March in Vermont. With temperatures below freezing, we knew food, water, and shelter were scarce, especially for a little animal who most likely hadn't grown up in the surrounding woods.

We set out a small dish of cat food and a bowl of water under the roof of our open-faced woodshed. By the next morning, the trail camera confirmed our little friend had managed to find the food and water, dining for over half an hour and sleeping all through the night in the cozy bed we'd made for him. It became clear he was more than just hungry and tired—he was sick and needed help.

After naming the cat Felix, caring for him quickly consumed our thoughts and energy in heart-captivating ways over the next couple of days. When we weren't making improvements to better insulate his little shelter or filling his dish with food, his sweet face glimmered in the forefront of our minds.

Getting to love Felix was the gentle balm that soothed our aching hearts. It united us and lit lanterns of joy, illuminating the darkness that had clouded our days.

When our neighbor mentioned he'd seen the same cat drinking out of a dirty puddle in his driveway a couple of weeks prior, it only confirmed our suspicions that Felix had been out on his own for a long time—*too long*. It had been a few days since his arrival and we still hadn't found his owner—we knew it was time to take him to the vet and get him the medical attention he so clearly needed.

We found Felix sleeping peacefully in his bed, hugging the little mouse toy we'd given him.

"Hi sweet boy," I spoke calmly, not wanting to startle him.

"We're going to get you the help you need to be healthy and strong," my husband said gently. After telling Felix how much we loved him, we noticed his ears hadn't been moving to the sound of our voices as cat ears typically do.

"I don't think he's breathing," my husband whispered under his breath.

My heart dropped into the pit of my stomach. *No, no—this can't be happening*, I thought to myself. We were going to be gardening buddies out in the yard all summer. He'd hear the slam of the screen door and come running to join us for an afternoon of weeding the garden and harvesting vegetables. He'd climb the pear tree and we'd smile up at his sweet face amongst the pear blossoms. He'd be healthy and strong—he'd curl up in our laps and doze off in the warmth of the sun.

He wasn't supposed to leave us now—not before we even got to hold him.

Not him too...

"I'm so sorry!" I cried, choking on the despair caught in my throat.

Why did he have to be taken away?

Why do we have to say goodbye?

At that moment, time stopped. In a slow-motion daze, we buried our sweet friend and said goodbye. Standing there in the middle of the woods, covered in dirt and snow, we let our hearts be shattered into thousands of little pieces. In our confusion, pain, anger, and helplessness, we clung to each other and cried until we could barely breathe.

Collapsing into our Father's arms, we finally, *finally* grieved.

For Felix. For our first little baby. For our second baby.

The ones we never got to hold.

The memories we never got to make.

The little lives we loved with all the love in our hearts.

It was as if the floodgates of grief opened at that very moment.

And God was there to hold us with a supernatural strength I'll never *ever* forget.

* * *

A dear friend once compared losing someone you love to standing ankle-deep in the ever-moving waves of the sea with your back to the water. Waves of grief come and go, rise and fall. You know there will be waves rolling in, but with your back to the sea, you don't know when—or how forceful they will be. In a split moment, stronger waves may supersede the lapping waters and shake your balance—*you may nearly lose your footing.* Other times, you may hardly feel the waves around your feet, numb to the cold, having stood in the waters of grief for so long.

And still, without warning, a giant squall may rise out of the sea, crashing into shore and knocking you off your feet. Engulfed in waves, you may find yourself completely wrecked, unsure how to get back up again.

That's where I'd found myself amid the grief of the past year—thrashing in the waves that felt too heavy to handle. I called out in honest cries and he heard me. God pulled me close and held me tight. In the days and weeks following Felix's loss, I remember experiencing this feeling of being gently rocked whenever I would come to God in prayer. In his arms, I was safe to feel the sorrow and hurt I'd numbed myself to push away. In humbled awe, I watched as God brought transformative healing into my life, carrying me out of utter brokenness into full restoration.

It's since become clear to me that when we're standing in the waves with our backs to the sea, God is standing there facing us—feet in the sand, arms stretched out ready to catch and hold us. He's ready to bring restorative healing in the darkest pockets of our lives. It's a wonder that can only be explained by the unfailing grace and love so great that even amid sorrow and loss, there can also be deep peace that surpasses all human understanding.

***

My husband and I often talk about how God knew Felix only had a few more days to live when he brought him into our lives. Why had he done that—letting us love so hard, only to lose *again*?

Had he known the joy it would bring us to love amid our numbness and grief—how tangibly caring for Felix would bring healing to our hearts?

Had God known that the physical act of burying Felix and saying goodbye would be the open door we so desperately needed to enter into fully grieving the babies we lost?

I believe he did.

I believe God cares about *every* detail of our lives.

And I believe he's there on the beach with us, arms open wide.

Meet the Writers

A. A. Kostas is a Canadian-Australian writer and lawyer, currently based in Singapore. His poetry, fiction, essays and reviews have appeared or are forthcoming in *The Clayjar Review, The Rialto Books Review*, and *Ekstasis*. You can read more of his work on Substack: https://waymarkers.substack.com/.

Abbi Bodager is a college student who is passionate about Jesus and storytelling. Her poetry has been published by *The Solitary Daisy* and *Ekstasis*. You can read more of her work by visiting her Substack, heavens declare.

Abigail Hofland is a wife, mother, and freelance writer raised in New York and most recently replanted in California. Her interests include music, missions, midwifery, and Micah (her handsome half).

Abigail Perez is a 'budding' poet and author, with *Calla Press* being the first place to officially publish one of her works. Abigail currently resides in Maine with her husband and mini-goldendoodle. When not writing (or reading, for that matter), she enjoys exploring New England and getting in touch with the beautiful nature God created there. Should you want to read more of her work, you can find it here on her Substack: https://aarpzz.substack.com.

Abigail Rainey is an interdisciplinary visual artist, poet, and arts educator from May, Texas. Spending part of her childhood moving across the U.S. and part of it in a tiny country town, her creative investigations stem from a consciousness of home, inheritance, restoration, and permanence. She is constantly inspired by the ways she sees God in her everyday life, in the most mundane moments, and much of her work draws on this overlap of the common and the sacred. Abi is currently based in Denton, Texas, where she enjoys teaching painting and drawing to students of all ages while she is finishing her Masters of Fine Arts in Visual Arts degree. She loves trying out new food trucks, sifting through a good used bookstore, and going on walks with her sweet husband Seth, who patiently waits while she takes photos of all the pretty light she sees along the way.

Adam Ryan Barton is a graduate student at the University of Dallas. He holds a Bachelor of Arts from Dallas Baptist University and a Master of Arts from Texas State University. His work has previously appeared in *Christianity and Literature*. Apart from writing, his greatest joy is spending time with his wife,

Caroline, their newborn son, Lucas, his dog, Josie, and his cat, Desdemona. He currently teaches at St. Joseph Catholic School in Arlington, Texas.

Alexis Ragan is a faith inspired, deep-image poet, or as she delights to think of it, a literary vessel for Christ's light to dwell, convinced that creative arts serve as a powerful window of worship that leads humanity back to the beauty of God's heart. As a seasoned ESL instructor who is passionate about poetry, music, storytelling, global outreach, and supporting mental health, she presently blends her love for creative writing and tutoring English in the collegial atmosphere. She created the literary journal, *Vessels of Light*, to live as a warm, virtual lighthouse that inspires souls through the gift of literary arts. Alexis has been published in places such as *Ekstasis, Calla Press, Alabaster Co, The Way Back To Ourselves*, and *Christianity Today*. She is currently pursuing an MFA in poetry at California State University Long Beach.

Ali Noël is a homeschool mama of three living in the rainy shadow of Mt. Rainier. She spends her time penning poems and sharing Middle Grade adventures on her Substack @alinoelwrites. She has spent the last year as a poetry intern for a small press publishing house, and holds a Bachelors of Science in Biblical Studies from Indiana Wesleyan University. Ali's work has been featured in *Learning Well Journal, Vessel of Light Journal*, and *Twenty Hills Publishing*.

Allana Walker is a writer and editor from the Canadian East Coast. She serves as the senior editor for Calla Press Publishing, LLC and runs a Substack blog titled "Daughter of the King." Allana loves literature, music, and fresh loaves of sourdough. For a taste of her writing, you are welcome to visit her blog at https://allanawalker.substack.com/.

Allison Moore Giles earned a B.A. in English from Grove City College in Grove City, PA and holds an M.A. in English from the University of Wisconsin-Milwaukee. She and her husband and three children serve as missionaries, and their hearts remain with a small community near Addis Ababa, Ethiopia, where they made their home for seven years. She and her family are relocating to Nairobi, Kenya where they will offer technical training as a means of discipleship, providing a way to make a living to nationals and the Ethiopian diaspora. Allison's writings have appeared in *The Way Back 2 Ourselves* and *The Clayjar Review*. You can find Allison on Substack @allisonmooregiles.

Aly Prades is a former ESL writing professor and current seeker of magic in the margins. She lives in North Idaho with her husband and two kids. She loves to craft words, and arts and crafts used to make her skin crawl, but now she's experimenting with watercolor and having...fun...gasp. She is a foodie who hates cooking and is always dancing the line between thoughtful introspection and overthinking. You can read more about her experience of growing up with undiagnosed OCD, as well as her poetry, newsletters, and pep talks at A Glitch in the Good Enough (https://alyprades.substack.com/), where she also offers many OCD recovery resources.

A.M. Everett is a former missionary-turned-Pastor's wife living in Oregon with her husband and three precious kids. "Mourning Light" was written for Henry, her first son, who was born with a rare genetic disability. The longer A.M. lives, the more confident she grows in the goodness and sovereignty of God! To Him be all the glory!

Amanda Nowlin is a less than perfect pastor's wife, a Registered Nurse turned homeschooling mom of four. She loves literature, nature and adventures of all kinds. She has struggled hard through doubt and depression and writes about the grace and love of a good God who sustains her through it all. You can read more of her work on her Substack: https://riversinthedesert.substack.com/.

Amandalea Rodriguez Noel is a follower of Jesus who embraces writing as an act of worship—a sacred space to offer her whole self and experience the transforming work of the Spirit. She teaches English and composition, encouraging her students to discover the dynamic power of words. With a Master's degree in Creative Writing, she writes about the beauty found in banal and broken things—believing that every moment, even the most ordinary ones, are filled with divine significance.

Amber Leigh Lipscomb views poetry as a form of devotional time with God, allowing her to communicate His messages through His ink. While faith is at the core of her writing, she also explores the complexities of human emotion—reflection, growth, and connection. She believes her pen is guided by God, shaping each word with purpose. For her, writing is not just self-expression, but a calling—a way to offer truth, comfort, and inspiration to others, trusting that even in the depths of uncertainty, God is always at work.

Ana Lauran: Growing up in Romania, Ana remembers starting to write poetry as soon as she learned to read and write, having fun with grade-school rhythms and rhymes in her native language. Over the years, though, she discovered that words are not bound by one language or culture: in 2016, she moved with her family from Romania to Portland, OR, a confused yet enthusiastic 7th grader who never stopped writing even when her whole world shifted. Ana is pursuing a career in Speech and Language Pathology because she loves people and communication, but her dream is to one day be a stay-at-home mom. Besides poetry, Ana enjoys joining others in their own hobbies, particularly in activities that involve watching movies, reading, traveling, experiencing live music and theater, trying foods from around the world, and exploring the gorgeous PNW. Her deepest passion is caring for people and walking with them toward Jesus.

April Ficklin is a former high school English teacher and mom of four teens whose family grew through adoption over eight years ago. She was able to passionately use her degrees in English and teaching credentials many years in traditional high schools, in online classes, and in college classrooms. But her love for learning and educating was transformed after entering the world of adoption and advocacy, and she now works as the Director of Family Services for a non-profit providing family coaching and support for other adoptive families. From developing classroom curricula to writing Bible studies for her local church to creating parenting sessions for online seminars, April has always been able to weave her writing, her desire of lifelong learning, her gift of teaching, and her faith into every professional endeavor.

Ashley Setterlind is a pastor's wife, mama to four little ones on earth + one in heaven, writer, and board-certified trauma-informed mental health coach. She is passionate about Biblical literacy and encouraging women to pursue healing and growth for the glory of God. Fancy iced lattes, wandering through bookstores, and deep chats around a fire are three of her favorite things. You can connect with her more on Instagram @ashleysetterlind.

Ashlyn McKayla Ohm: A worshiper of the Creator and a wanderer of creation, Ashlyn McKayla Ohm is the author of the contemporary fiction *Climbing Higher* trilogy as well as devotional and poetry collections. Her work has been featured in *Clayjar Review, Truly Co., Proverbs 31, Vessels of Light*, and *Heart of Flesh*. If she's not reading or writing, she's probably hiking, birdwatching, or otherwise getting lost in the woods. Follow Ashlyn's adventures at wordsfromthewilderness.substack.com.

Awara Fernández lives in Georgia with her husband of 35 years and their rescue dog, Gonzo. They have 6 children and 8 grandchildren, and Awara loves being Nana! You can find more of her writing at kosmeomag.com, valiantscribe.com, herviewfromhome.com, theway back2ourselves.com, markinc.org, and anunexpectedjounal.com. You can find her at facebook.com/awara.fernandez.

Bailey Gillespie is a writer from Northern California. After a career in higher education and publishing, she now hosts a podcast called Listen to Your Life and cares deeply about helping others walk in hope and well-being. Besides writing, she enjoys road trips to the coast, farmers markets, and cooking with her husband Noah (and their orange tabby, Chef). Bailey has written on art, women's health, and spiritual formation for *Inkwell* (formerly *Ekstasis Magazine*), *IAPMD Global, She Reads Truth*, and *The Rabbit Room*. You can follow her on Instagram @baileylgillespie and on Substack at baileygillespie.substack.com.

Bernadette Lamb is an author and illustrator based in St. Louis, Missouri. Her work for young people often deals with relational healing, the fantastical, and the complicated business of growing up. Like the keeper of a lighthouse, she wants to guide her readers to shore. When she's not telling stories, you'll probably find her re-watching *The Incredibles* or in a thrift store searching for the latest addition to her library. See Bernadette online at bernadettelamb.com or on Instagram as @thejoyfulbear.

Bethany Colas is a poet, military spouse, and mother of three who currently resides in the suburbs of Connecticut. When Bethany's not writing poems in the margins of her days, she can be found reading mystery novels from the Golden Age era and drinking tea. Her poems have been published in *Ekstasis Magazine, The Rabbit Room Poetry Substack, The Way Back to Ourselves*, and *Clayjar Review*. She also belongs to the fellowship of writers at Cultivating Oaks Press.

Bethany Peck is a writer and photographer living near the beautiful Chesapeake Bay in northeastern Maryland. She loves nature and writes about experiencing God's love through creation at bethanypeck.org and on Instagram at @beautiful_purpose_writing. She's been featured in *Fathom Magazine, The Way Back to Ourselves, The ClayJar Review*, and other outlets. She and her dog Hunter stay active by hiking, paddleboarding, and enjoying long evening walks.

Bethany Valyou is the writer and creator of *On the Winding Path*, a reflective blog devoted to finding peace and renewal through faith and the rhythms of seasonal living. She shares devotionals, reflections, and creative resources to encourage readers to slow down, find hope in God, and discover joy in everyday moments. Bethany lives in the mountains of Vermont with her husband and works as a copywriter, helping artists and authors authentically share their stories and visions. Connect with her at onthewindingpath.com.

Brianna Marshall is a pastor's kid, a sister to two sisters, and a recently graduated high school senior. She grew up in the Midwest and loves to express herself in creative ways, like writing, painting, and crafting.

Caitlin Callahan is a writer and illustrator. She earned her B.A. in writing from Point Loma Nazarene University, and she has published poetry with *Calla Press Publishing, Quirk, Seasonal Fruits Literary Magazine*, and *Driftwood*. She also self-published a comic book called *Korina: The King's Own*. Currently, you can find her on Instagram, LinkedIn, and Substack.

Caitlin Lore is a Midwest grown, Southeast transplant who often writes about the interplay of faith, grief, and midlife on her Substack, *The Time Given*. A former English teacher, she also writes children's fiction and has a middle grade short story forthcoming from Twenty Hills. In her free time, Caitlin is rarely without a book, enjoys gardening, and dabbles in several eclectic hobbies which inevitably end up in her stories. Find her online @caitlin_lore or caitlinlore.com.

Calli Shea Birch is an English literature and writing educator with over a decade of experience spanning classrooms in London, Dallas, and Little Rock. After choosing to homeschool her own daughters, Calli dreamed of creating a space where students could join their stories with those classic tales that point hearts and minds toward things that are beautiful, good, and true. In 2023 she launched Storyweaver Co., a curated home education platform that offers à la carte English classes for middle & high school students. In Storyweaver literature courses, Calli's students learn the art of reading well, open their eyes to see and value other perspectives, and develop courageous voices in their written expression. As a VELA founder and educational grant recipient, Calli strives to provide a rich resource for creative and innovative homeschooling families. You can find her at storyweaverco.com and on Instagram @storyweaverco.

Camilla Richardson: Hailing from Arizona, Camilla draws inspiration from her native desert and the lush green of Germany, where she had the pleasure of living and studying. She holds her bachelor's in Liberal Studies and is a freelance writer, recently appearing in *Business Insider, Her View From Home, The Way Back to Ourselves, Blue Flame Review*, and more. You can currently find her combing through archives for a historical fiction based in India. Follow her on Substack @camillarichardsonwriter for more.

Caroline Liberatore is a poet, editor, and librarian from Cleveland, Ohio. Her vocations indicate what she cares most deeply for: the written word, artistic excellence, embodied presence in local communities, commonplace beauty, and the tangible redemption of Christ. Caroline serves as Editor at *The Clayjar Review* and writes regularly on her Substack, *Dog-Eared Inquiries*.

Carolyn Etzel Branch lives in Durham, NC with her husband, where she is pursuing an MDiv from Duke Divinity School with certificates in Theology & the Arts and Anglican Studies. Her creative writing has been featured in *Ekstasis* and *The ClayJar Review*, and more can be found at her substack, *The Rewilding Script*.

Casey Sorensen is a poet and writer residing in southeast Michigan with her husband and two sons. She is a lover of Jesus, organizing, and sending cards via snail mail. Casey's work has been published in *Her View From Home* and *Compel Pro*. Casey also contributes monthly to the locally-focused parenting resource *Detroit Mom*. Feel free to read more of her work pertaining to faith, encouragement and motherhood @words.with.casey.

Chanda Singleton Griesë seeks everyday glimmers of grace in the ordinary, penning hope with the revelation of the unseen. Growing up in Florida, she marveled at the wonders of nature. As a mother, she learned to recapture those moments with her children in visits to parks and preserves, springs and beaches. Chanda resides in the central Florida area with her husband, four children, and two tabby cats. She also writes on her blog, Everyday Grace, at chandagriese.substack.com.

Charis Crandall lives in Wembley, Alberta, Canada and enjoys exploring the northern prairies and mountains of this land she calls home. Her appreciation for God's grace in both the ordinary and difficult moments of life is reflected in her art and her writing. She can be found on Instagram as @charisdcrandall and Substack at charisdcrandall.substack.com.

Charissa Sylvia is a poet pilgrim, pastor's wife and mama writing in real, extraordinary time from the high desert of New Mexico. Her poems have appeared in *Ekstasis Magazine, The Rabbit Room, Calla Press, The Fallow House,* and *The Windhover.* She is the creator and host of #twentywordtuesday, a weekly short-form writing challenge hosted on social media. You can read more of her poetry and other writing on her Substack: Reason & Rhyme.

Chelsea Fraser is a wife, mother, poet, musician, and arts administrator who has been published in *Ekstasis Magazine, The Dewdrop, Vessels of Light Journal, Persephone Literary Magazine,* and *The Way Back to Ourselves Literary Journal.* Her debut poetry collection, *The Mother Tree,* released in spring 2025 through "vine & shoots publishing." She has been a featured poet at Inkwell creative gatherings.

Cheryl Eichman is a passionate follower of God who desires for people to live loved by the Lord. Cheryl is a wife, mom, daughter, friend, writer, artist, and nature-lover. When she is not writing, she can be found exploring the mountains, grabbing a cup of coffee, capturing beauty with her camera, painting in her messy room, or caring for her dear mom. You can find her on Instagram @ cheryl.eichman, or on Substack https://substack.com/@cheryleichman.

Christel Jeffs is a writer, editor, and counselor. She lives in Northland, New Zealand, the place that serves as the backdrop for her debut novel, *The Gumdigger's Wife* (2016). Her poetry has been featured in *Fast Fibres Poetry, The Way Back To Ourselves* and *Vessels of Light.* She loves to help others re-write their stories through her counseling work while continuing to author her own, guided by the greatest Storyteller of all.

Christina Snyder is mom to two young boys and spends her days tending to their hearts and lives. Together with her husband, they make their home in wild Idaho with their families. She is honored to have her works in *Calla Press'* spring journal for a second year in a row. More of her liturgies and poetry can be found at christinasnyder.substack.com.

Christy Lynne Wood spent her teens and early twenties in a Christian cult, but Jesus found her anyway. More than twenty years later, Christy continues to pick apart legalism, twisted Scripture, and lies in a search for the truth. As a speaker, podcaster, writer, and author of *Religious Rebels: Finding Jesus in the Awkward Middle Way of Grace and Truth* (2023), she is passionate about helping people to find a genuine relationship with Jesus. Christy lives in West Michigan with her wonderfully-opposite husband and their two children.

Civil Winters lives in the heart of the Canadian prairies where she designs regenerative landscapes. When her hands aren't full of earth or earl grey tea, she runs, writes, paints, chases her niece and entertains an ark-load of critters. Find her on Substack at https://www.substack.com/@driftverse.

Courtney Moody is a dancer, writer, and poet. Her prose and poetry have appeared in publications such as *Bridge Eight, Propertius Press,* and *Ekstasis Magazine.* In 2022, her poem "Florida Anatomy" was awarded 2nd place for the Florida State Poet's Association Award, and in 2024, she was invited to contribute to *Christianity Today's* Advent devotional, *A Time for Wonder.* She currently acts as Assistant Editor for the *Vessels of Light* literary journal while dancing and writing in the heat of the sunshine state. She can be found on Instagram @ courtofwriting.

Cyndy Chisare is a retired technical librarian and graphic designer who believes in the miraculous of the everyday. Since her retirement from both an academic and research library in New York, she has resettled to the Shenandoah Valley of Virginia where she has learned to live by the seasons and embrace a slowed-down life. She likes to spend her days in the Blue Ridge Mountains with her family, hiking trails, watching wildlife and listening to the stories of the mountains. Cyndy collects old books, old photos and ephemera that speak of human history and stories that are waiting to be told. She firmly believes that all things are possible with God and that He is always showing her a "new thing". She can be reached at her email: cchisare@gmail.com

Dabney Baldridge is a busy mother of three boys who writes in the middle of life's messiness to create beauty out of chaos. Her work has been published in *America's Best Emerging Poets* and *Pennsylvania's Best Emerging Poets* by Z Publishing House. When she is not writing, Dabney dabbles in photography and art and loves getting lost somewhere in the woods with her boys.

Dana Portillo: Originally from the Deep South, Dana currently writes from her urban Indiana home, where a searching eye for beauty in all places grounds her to what is true. Although she is new to the published world of writing, she has been expressing herself through the written word from a young age. As a trained visual artist and designer, she enjoys many other forms of creative expression, including flower arranging, knitting, and cooking. She is passionate about group Bible studies and long, theological dives. Dana is happily married and homeschools her four children with a heavy focus on good literature (of course). She proudly carries on a family tradition of dachshund ownership, and she best describes herself as an introverted Anne Shirley.

Daniel Bishop is in the business of words that rumble the earth like giant fists of hail. His work has appeared in *Ekstasis*, *The Penwood Review*, and *Prometheus Dreaming*. You can read more of his prose and poetry on Substack: @ BishopoftheEastWind.

Danielle Page is a truth-teller, writer, educator, and editor of the *Clayjar Review*. When she's not reading up on composition theory, she's scribbling in her moleskine journal or hiking a mountainous trail. Her work has appeared in *Solid Food Press*, *The Amethyst Review*, *Ekstasis Magazine*, and elsewhere.

Deborah Rutherford, a writer and poet, explores themes of faith, nature, healing, and grace. She is the founder of the Behold-Her Beauty Blog & Podcast. Her published works are in the books *Unexpected Blessings: 40 Days of Discovering God's Best* and *Prodigal Daughter: poems of light for lost ones*, published by The Way Back Books Fall 2025, and publications *The Way Back to Ourselves Journal*, *Vessels of Light Journal*, *Calla Press Literary Journal Spring*, *The Truly Co. Magazine*, *Austur Magazine*, *Aletheia Today Magazine*, and *Prosetrics Literary Magazine*. At heart, Deborah loves sharing her many stories, singing old hymns, and taking long walks in the woods, where she finds inspiration and peace. You can find her at www.deborahrutherford.com, https://deborahrutherford.substack.com/ and Instagram @deborahrutherfordwrites.

Debra Fair is a high school English teacher by day and a writer by night. As an author, she specializes in poetry and creative nonfiction centered on faith, nature, and mental health. Outside of work and writing, she is a passionate equestrian and spends most of her free time caring for her horse and miniature donkey. For more of her work, follow @fair.minded.poetry on Instagram and Facebook.

Donna Bucher is a poet, author, speaker, experienced counselor and hospice and palliative care support personnel and founder of Serenity in Suffering blog and Substack. Her writings have appeared in various online sites as well as *Prosetrics Magazine*, *Austur Magazine*, *Aletheia Today*, *Calla Press*, *Vessels of Light*, and *The Way Back to Ourselves Literary Journals*. Donna also has a published devotional through Arabelle Publishing. You can connect with her on her Substack, https://serenityinsuffering.substack.com/.

Dorothy Nielsen's poems have been featured in many U.S. and Canadian journals including *Christianity and Literature*, *Ekstasis*, *The Literary Review of Canada*, and *The Dalhousie Review*. She is the author of one poetry collection. Her essays appear in many books as well as in academic or literary journals, such as *Denise Levertov: New Perspectives*, *Contemporary Literature*, *Traces Journal*, and the forthcoming *The Alchemy of Stories: Essays on Literature and Life*.

Elizabeth Wickland lives in Bozeman, Montana with her husband, daughter, and two Yorkies. She has a love for words and their stories and has responded to life through poetry and art for as long as she can remember. She also enjoys gardening and cultivating beauty in her small corner of the world, whether in person or online. She writes for *The Black Barn Online*, and her work has been published in *The Unmooring, The Way Back to Ourselves, and The Rabbit Room* Poetry Substack, among others. You can find her on Instagram at @punamulta. priory and at elizabethwickland.substack.com.

Emily Boulter writes on faith, mountains, and the stories that shape us on her substack, "Alpine Penned." She has a BA in English and Writing from Regent University, loves helping veterans through a nonprofit she helped start called "Mountains Move," and can usually be found sipping coffee and reading a book at one of the local coffee shops. Her favorite books are children's books, and she still believes that Narnia is most definitely real.

Emma Michael is a wife, mother, and homeopath residing in Utah. Reading and writing poetry has been one of her lifelong joys, and she is grateful to Calla Press for the opportunity to share some of her words with you, to the glory of God.

Gloriaea is the author of *For Those in the Midst of It*, a debut collection of poetry and reflections published in 2024. She finds immense joy in the written word, and in the Word. You can find some of her work here (https://gloriaea. substack.com)

Gina Gallagher is married to her high school sweetheart. She is the mama of five grown children and the grandma of six precious grandchildren, with another one on the way. Gina loves reading, as her overflowing bookshelves can attest. She has always loved to write. Gina just published her first children's book, *Reading With Remmy*, with Calla Press in December. She began writing a devotional blog, *Whispers of His Movement*, in 2012 and still publishes weekly.

Hannah Grace Staton is first and finally a beloved daughter of the King. She is a homeschool graduate, student in the Young Writer's Workshop, and managing editor at Skillful Pen Press. Hannah Grace seeks to bring her faith to the page in fresh and creative ways, sharing what the Lord has been teaching her in a form others can benefit from. Memoirs, devotionals, and inspirational stories fill her shelves; Christians' songs from the 1990s and 2010s form the soundtrack of her life; and scribbled ideas of her own (often drawn from others' stories and songs) bubble into folders in her desk and eventually overflow into her writing. Her work has been featured by a few publications, including *Calla Press*, *Kosmeo* Magazine, and Beyond the Bookery. You can read more from Hannah Grace on her blog, the-grace-space.net.

Hannah May Schramm lives in Indiana, and she is a senior in high school. She loves reading, crafting, traveling with her family of five, and all things beautiful. Hannah is going to college to become an elementary teacher.

Hannah Sanders is a follower of Christ, wife, mom, teacher, artist and writer. She loves all things book-ish, afternoon tea, and growing things that bring butterflies and hummingbirds to her yard. She is happiest in the mountains and when surrounded by tall trees.

Heather Cadenhead's poems and essays have been featured in *Ekstasis Magazine*, *The Rabbit Room*, *Valley Voices*, *WILD + FREE*, *Reformed Journal*, *Foundling Review*, *Relief: A Journal of Art and Faith*, *The Clayjar Review*, *Radix Magazine*, *Mothers Always Write*, *Birmingham Arts Journal*, and other publications. Previously, she was a recipient of the New Plains Review Editorial Prize. Her poem, "Illiterate," was nominated for Best of the Net. She lives in Tennessee with her husband and their two children.

Henry Lewis a poet, novelist, and essayist living in the Minneapolis area with his lovely wife. He is a dawn-watcher, a night-sky-gazer, and a sojourner in a strange land. His work has appeared in *Veritas Journal*, *Ekstasis Magazine*, *Story Warren*, *The Clayjar Review*, and others. He has self-published two nonfiction books and frequently publishes essays on his substack A Curious Light.

Holli Gibbs enjoys life in east Tennessee. She has a B.A. and M.S. in Biblical Counseling, and she has worked in Christian camp and preschool settings since college. In her spare time, she coauthors the literary blog Melenoria and writes from personal experience in her substack newsletter Gratefully Single. You can follow her writing journey at holligibbs.com.

Isabel Chenot has loved, memorised, and practised poetry all her remembered life. Some of her poems are collected in *The Joseph Tree*, and recently poems have appeared or are forthcoming in places like *Brazen Head*, *Voegelin View*, *Trampoline*, *Amethyst*.

James Robert Kibby is a songwriter and poet whose love for creative writing began when he authored and illustrated his first comic book at age 11. James has poems published through *Calla Press*, *The Voices Project*, *Amethyst Review*, and *Agape Review*. James is a devoted husband, father, and deacon at his church.

Jana Carlson is a freelance writer, Bible teacher, and writing mentor with a mission to inspire women and writers to love the Bible, "rightly handle the word of truth" (2 Tim 2:15), and wield the word for God's glory. She serves as a blog coordinator, editor, and women's ministry leader at her church. Connect with her at janacarlson.com.

Jen Niemann's love for writing returned during the Pandemic. Jen is a wife, mom, nurse, caregiver, and volunteers in her Women's Ministry and two other writing groups. She lives near the beautiful village of Chagrin Falls, Ohio. Find her sharing Soul Singings on Substack at jenniemann.substack.com.

Judy Swartz is a recently retired great-grandmother enjoying her newfound freedom to spend more time with a book or a pen in her hands. Writing has long been her means of the continual emptying of her heart so God can keep refilling it. She and her husband of 38 years enjoy time with their family, traveling, and gardening.

Julia McMullen is a writer living in Nebraska with her husband and their two young children. She loves spending time in nature and meditating on the beauty of God's creation. Her work has appeared most recently in *The Way Back to Ourselves Journal* and *Clayjar Review*.

Justin Farley is a poet and author from Indianapolis, Indiana USA. He has been published in journals such as *The Ekphrastic Review, Calla Press*, and *wrkwndr*. He has released five collections of poetry, with a new release due shortly, all available on Amazon. Follow him on instagram @justinfarleypoet.

Justin Lonas is a writer (jryanlonas.substack.com), cook, amateur naturalist, art-lover, and semi-professional theologian (MDiv) from Chattanooga, Tennessee. By day, he serves at the Chalmers Center at Covenant College. His poems, essays, and reviews have appeared in *Fathom, Ekstasis, Englewood Review of Books, Fallow House, The Walnut Branch, Mere Orthodoxy*, and *The Gospel Coalition*.

Karen Swallow Prior, Ph. D., is a reader, writer, and speaker. She is the author of *You are Called: Finding your Vocation in the True, Good, and Beautiful* (Brazos 2025). *The Evangelical Imagination: How Stories, Images, and Metaphors Created a Culture in Crisis* (Brazos 2023); *On Reading Well: Finding the Good Life through Great Books* (Brazos 2018); *Fierce Convictions: The Extraordinary Life of Hannah More—Poet, Reformer, Abolitionist* (Thomas Nelson 2014); and *Booked: Literature in the Soul of Me* (T. S. Poetry Press 2012). She is co-editor of *Cultural Engagement: A Crash Course in Contemporary Issues* (Zondervan 2019) and has contributed to numerous other books. She has a monthly column for *Religion News Service*. Her writing has appeared at *Christianity Today, New York Times, The Atlantic, The Washington Post, First Things, Vox, Think Christian, The Gospel Coalition*, and various other places. She hosted the podcast *Jane and Jesus*.

Karyn Hunt is a poet, lyricist, and follower of Jesus who views her writing as a ministry. She holds a B.A. in English from SUNY Geneseo. She also attended Niagara University. She lives near St. Louis, MO, with her husband and son. In addition to writing, Karyn enjoys reading, playing board games, and spending time in nature. You can find more of her writing at karynhuntwrites.com.

Kathy Young is a writer who resides in central Florida with her high school sweetheart and daughter. An avid reader and nature trail explorer, she loves to write about what it means to live a quietly faithful life and press into silent, still moments. You can connect with Kathy on her Substack, Less Noise, Low Whispers.

Kelli Sallman freelances in Overland Park, Kansas, as a writer, editor, and writing mentor. Coauthor or ghostwriter of several books, she holds a Master of Theology degree from Dallas Theological Seminary. She has work forthcoming in *Relief* and writes poetry that explores human experience, especially experiences of loss and chronic illness, through a lens of faith.

Kelly Hellmuth is an author and poet who resides in Norman, Oklahoma with her husband and four children. When she's not crafting with words, she teaches high school literature, working to instill a love of storytelling in future generations. She also is enrolled in Duke Divinity School, where she is pursuing her Masters in Divinity, hoping to place her focus on the intersection between theology and the arts.

Kelly Meagher is a writer and contemplative poet whose work both in writing and leading creative retreats always aims to see the Kingdom of God grow and bring others closer to the heart of their Savior. You can connect with more of Kelly's work through her poetry book, *When He Whispers Your Name*, or through her podcast, *The Til*.

Kenzie McGregor is a word lover from South Carolina who searches for the hauntingly beautiful in life, art, and faith. She aspires to follow the literary footsteps of Flannery O'Connor while bringing hope and light to others through her work.

Kimberly Phinney is a professor and writer. She's published in *Christianity Today, Ekstasis, Fathom, Solum*, and more. A doctoral candidate, she holds her M.Ed. in English and was featured on *Good Morning America* for a national educator award. She was recently nominated for the Pushcart Prize, and her poetry collections, *Of Wings and Dirt* and *Exalted Ground*, debuted as #1 on Amazon in Christian Poetry in 2024 and 2025. Visit her community at www. TheWayBack2Ourselves.com.

Kris Ann Valdez is an Arizona native, wife, and mother to three children. Her work appears in *Ekstasis, Clay Jar Press*, and *So God Made a Grandma* by Tyndale House Publishers. She also has two middle-grade novels forthcoming with Twenty Hills Press. Follow her on Substack as "The Guide Girl" or on Instagram @krisannvaldezwrites or her pen name (fiction) @annvalwrites

Kristen Avila: Passionate about transforming how we experience pain in all of its forms, Kristen Avila believes we are as beautifully broken by God as we are created. She lives in Sonoma County, California where she spends her free time with family in nature.

Kristine Amundrud is a poet of faith from Alberta, Canada, who enjoys exquisite views of the majestic Canadian Rockies. Her family will soon call Northland, New Zealand home. She finds joy in dreaming alongside her husband, and their three children. Inspired by nature and story work, Kristine endeavors to stir up emotion in the reader. She is a Pushcart Prize Nominee for her poem, "Anemone Blue." You can read more of her work at: www.kristineamundrud.substack.com, or on Instagram: @kamundrud

Laura Vogt is a historian and storyteller. Her poetry is published in various journals, including *Fourteen Hills*, *Pleiades*, and *Enchanted Living*, and she attended the University of Iowa Writers' Workshop in Dublin, Ireland. Her debut novel In the Great Quiet, a sweeping, romantic wild west adventure based on her ancestor, is forthcoming winter 2026 from Lake Union.

Lauren Carrizal is a wife, mom, and writer living in Fort Worth, TX. Seeking to find holy ground in ordinary places, her writing encourages Christian women that hard things aren't the end of their story—they are what give their stories meaning. You can connect with Lauren on Instagram @laurencarrizal or read more of her work at laurencarrizal.substack.com.

Lauren Madsen lives with her husband and four children in Utah. She loves photography, family history, dark chocolate, and spending time in the sunshine. Recently her poems have appeared in the *Vessels of Light* and *The Way Back to Ourselves* literary journals. Through both the written and spoken word, Lauren hopes to encourage others along the path of faith. While spiritual topics are often the focus of her writing, she also enjoys eliciting a chuckle or two at her monthly poetry group gatherings.

Lea Emmett is a wife, mom, and nurse residing in the suburbs of Chicago. She loves Jesus and is passionate about people learning the depths and riches of the gospel. She hopes her poetry will encourage readers to think deeply about God's character.

Lee Kiblinger is a Texas poet who loves to travel, laugh with three adulting children, play mahjong, and enjoy words with Rabbit Room poets. Her work can be found in *Calla Press, The Windhover, Solum Journal, Heart of Flesh, Ekstasis, Clayjar Review*, and others. Her first book, *All the Untils*, has just been published by Wipf and Stock. You can read more of her poetry at www.ripplesoflaughter.com.

Leilani Mueller is a California native and Texas transplant. You will often find her with one of her favorite people—her professor husband and her five little ones. When she isn't busy keeping up with her children (and large dog), you will find her with a book in hand or her fingers on the keyboard. She is also an avid coffee drinker, something of an anglophile, and still loves a spin on a bicycle. When not homeschooling her children, or teaching British Literature, she may be thinking about theater directing, a job in which she still dabbles. She is the author of *All Aboard the Grandparents Express* and she has written for *First Things*. You can find her on instagram at @leiraewrites.

Lindsey Gallant is a writer and poet based in Prince Edward Island, Canada. She loves small wonders, big ideas, good books, ditch flowers, and attending to the presence of God in ordinary life. Find her poetry and prose at lindseygallant.com.

Lisa M. Johnson is a retired pastor's wife, now full time "Lolly," the Italian grandmother of three, mentor and writer. In the past few years, Lisa has dedicated herself to discovering rest, healthy rhythms and healing through grief therapy, story work and time in her secret garden. You can find her in the quiet outside her home in the heart of the Bluegrass in Versailles, KY sipping a cup of hot tea waiting for you to join her. Other published works included in *The Way Back To Ourselves Literary Journal* and *Publish Her Press Anthology*. Connect on Instagram: @lisamicelijohnson

Liza Moore is an artist who resides with her husband and son in Round Rock, TX. She has created three children's books, and some of her artwork, poetry, and essays have been published in various journals including *Fathom Mag, Ekstasis Magazine, EcoTheo Review, Apple Valley Review, Thimble Literary Magazine, St. Katherine Review,* and *Humana Obscura*. To learn more about Liza and her creative work, please visit: https://campsite.bio/liza_moore_art.

Liz Jakimow is an Australian writer, poet and photographer who lives in the beautiful town of Araluen in Australia. Her poems, articles and photographs have appeared in multiple publications, including *Gossamer Arts, Art/s and Theology* and *Dulcet Literary Review*. She has self-published a book titled *She Thinks of Jesus*, which is a collection of short stories told from the point of view of women who witnessed the events in the gospels. You may read Liz's blog at https://substack.com/@edenslight.

Lucien Levant is a Southern California-based writer and office worker. His influences include other professionals-turned-writers such as ETA Hoffmann, Wallace Stevens, and Dana Gioia. Lucien enjoys studying the Word and classic films, and visiting family in the South, all themes that he often incorporates into his writing. Lucien is currently pursuing a master's degree at Pepperdine University and occasionally posts his shorter poems on his Instagram account @jigsandfixtures.

Luke Waggoner is an author who writes about faith, politics, his travels, and the mundane, both fiction and nonfiction. He's published research and miscellany in *The Washington Post, Christianity Today*, and elsewhere. He lives in Nashville with his wife and daughter. You can find his musing at https://luke-waggoner.substack.com/.

Mariellen Van Nieuwenhuyzen is a small-town family medicine physician in southwest Idaho. Outside of medicine she has a strong passion for writing and her work has frequently been featured in *Core Christianity, In All Things, Christianity Today*, and other online faith-based publications and literary magazines. Raised on a close-knit family farm and apiary in Northern California, she has a strong passion for the intersection of faith, agriculture, creation renewal, and membership in community. She is always striving to find a whimsical balance between sharing new adventures with husband, practicing medicine, writing, farming, and exploring God's beautiful creation.

Marilyn R. Gardner is a writer and public health nurse living in Boston. She loves weaving words and stories, as well as partnering with communities and health care systems to bridge gaps in communication and care. Her biggest achievement is birthing and raising five children on three continents, and now enjoying the deep friendships they share as adults. She has published two books, *Between Worlds: Essays on Culture and Belonging* and *Worlds Apart: A Third Culture Kid's Journey*. Her work has also appeared in *Plough, Fathom,* and *Among Worlds Magazines,* the *Calla Press Literary Journal,* and in chapters of three other books.

Mark Rico writes poetry because his mother showed him how to see—and his father showed him how to live intentionally. His work has most recently appeared in *Clayjar Review.* Mark lives in Chattanooga, TN, with his wife, Amy, and their four children. He writes at https://mimesiskinesis.substack.com.

Mary Anne Abdo is an author, poet and photographer. She graduated magna cum laude from Luzerne County Community College with a degree in Human Services. She has been featured in many print poetry magazines and anthologies. You can find more of her work in her self-published poetry book, *Fractured Lollipop Poems of Brokenness Healing and Hope,* and her children's book, *Pumpkin The Cat Who Plays With Words.* Both books are on Amazon. You may check out her work on: Facebook: Mary Anne Abdo/Poet/Author; or at Word Press: https://bluestainedglass.wordpress.com. Mary Anne resides in Scranton Pennsylvania.

Mary Madeline Schumpert is an essayist, poet, and wannabe painter. She lives in Birmingham, Alabama with her husband, Kyle, who makes her endless cappuccinos. She writes for ordinary artists and starry-eyed theologians, and you can find her work on Substack and Instagram, @mmschumpert.

Mary McReynolds, 78, is an author/poet living with her husband of 47 years in NW Arkansas. She writes verse on an almost daily basis and is never short of subject matter, thanks be to God. She has written three novels and one non fiction book. Her poetry collection is published under the title *Seeds and Stems*. An illustrated childrens' book is in production for release in the Fall, 2025.

Mckenzie Hunt is a mom, writer, and music therapist who prefers to be outside, relishing "the feast of creation." From a young age, she has kept a daily practice of journaling through which she has found space on the page to wrestle with God, befriend grief, and vivify her imagination for spiritual realities. She writes to invite and equip readers to faithfully steward their souls—the sacred soil she believes God has given each of us to keep. Mckenzie's writing has been published in *The Way Back to Ourselves* and *Vessels of Light* literary journals. You can find Mckenzie on Instagram @mckenzie.elizabeth.hunt, or on her Substack: Mckenziehunt.substack.com.

Megan Huwa is a poet and writer in southern California. A rare health condition keeps her and her husband from living near her family's five-generation farm in Colorado, so her writing reaches for home—both temporal and eternal. Her debut poetry collection, *Still Life* (Wipf & Stock), is forthcoming in fall 2025. Her work has been published in *Relief, Thimble, Vita Poetica, Solum Literary Press, Ekstasis*, and elsewhere. Find her at meganhuwa.com & @meganhuwa.

Megan Willome is the author of *Love and other Mysteries*, a poetry collection inspired by Song of Solomon and the twenty mysteries of the rosary. Her work has been featured at *Every Day Poems, Solum Journal, The Way Back to Ourselves*, and *The Windhover*. Her day is incomplete without poetry, tea, and a walk in the dark.

Melissa Alvarado Sierra is a Puerto Rican writer, poet, and editor living between Puerto Rico and the US Virgin Islands. Her work explores memory, myth, and the emotional geographies of island life. She has been published in *The New York Times, Orion Magazine, Catapult Magazine, Atticus Review*, and elsewhere. A graduate of the University of Barcelona and SNHU's Mountainview MFA program, she is currently pursuing a Ph.D. in Caribbean literature. Melissa is also the co-founder of *rhizomag*, a literary journal rooted in transmutation, grief, and the natural world. She is at work on a poetry collection and a novel.

Meredith Chester is a writer based in Chattanooga, Tennessee. She treasures time with God, The Grove writing group, her family, dear friends and her lovable goldendoodle. She holds a BA in English with a concentration in creative writing from Florida State University. Her flash fiction and poetry have appeared in the *Wilderness House Literary Review, La Piccioletta Barca, Assignment Literary Magazine's Micromag*, and *The Clayjar Review*. She also writes on Substack at https://meredithchester.substack.com.

Michelle Stankos is a former elementary school teacher turned author. She has written and published two children's picture books and recently started a podcast. Michelle loves to travel, attend concerts, and read. Michelle has two adult daughters and lives in Orlando, Florida with her husband.

M.L. Cole is a writer, graphic designer, and mystic at heart with a passion for all things hopeful and wholesome. She creates content on faith, mental health, creative lifestyle, and finding peace amid heartache at thebeaconroad. com and on Substack. Her poetry collection, *Altars in the Wilderness*, is available on Amazon.

Nancy Carroll: A spiritual director and writer, Nancy Carroll teaches, leads retreats, and loves to connect people more deeply with Christ through Scripture, storytelling, community, and contemplative spiritual practices. She has published several Bible studies. She helped found and is president emeritus of InSpero, Inc., a non-profit organization that cultivates hope and meaning for artists, churches, and the people of Birmingham, Alabama, by caring for its creatives and organizing opportunities for them to share their beautiful gifts with the city. She received her Master of Theological Studies from Beeson Divinity School and spiritual direction certification from Richmont Graduate University. Now that their two adult children have launched, she and her husband are enjoying their "Wonder Years" with two golden retrievers. Learn more at nancywcarroll.com.

Nikki Hurt is a pastor's wife, mother of five, and a creative writing teacher who lives and writes in northern Indiana. She is currently pursuing an MA in English at Eastern Illinois University and has been published by *Calla Press, The Vehicle, Family Life* and more. You can follow her writing at @author_nikki. hurt.

Olivia Oster is a writer living on Lookout Mountain, GA, whose fiction and poetry explore the spiritual aspect of common everyday life as well as the elements of life with which she is most familiar: chronic pain, parenting, writing, the Bible, and homemaking. Olivia's poetry has been accepted in *As Surely as the Sun, Spirit Fire Review* and others. She has also published *A New Grammary*, a book of grammar formulas, and a poetry chapbook called *Poetic Faith*. Olivia is a teacher, wife, mother of five, and student of the Word.

Ollie Burgess is a college student and piano teacher. She lives in a small town west of Atlanta's cityscape. If you cannot find her, just follow the trail of books throughout the house, or check to see if she's cloud-gazing on the trampoline again. If found at her desk, she is probably writing poetry for the lovers of strange cathedrals and enchanted forests. You can amble through her poetry gallery by visiting her Substack, *olivet* (olivetpoetry.substack.com).

Pat Severin is a retired Christian school teacher who finds poetic inspiration in her love of God. In addition to *Calla Press*, Pat has been published in *The Agape Review, the Clayjar Review, The Way Back 2 Ourselves*, and *Vessels of Light*, just to name a few. Her personal ministry is weekly sending cards with her poems of encouragment to those going through difficult life struggles.

Rachael Maddox is a writer passionate about exploring faith, love, and redemption through storytelling. When not writing, she can be found trying to put a dent in an ever-growing to-read list or enjoying a long run. She lives in Georgia with her husband and daughter.

Rachel Lynne Sakashita is a full-time Japanese language student and part-time intercultural ministry worker living with her husband in Pennsylvania. Her work can be found in blogs and journals such as *The Truly Co., Heart of Flesh Literary Journal, The Clayjar Review*, and her Substack, Ewe and Shepherd. Find her on Instagram at @abrightaubade.

Sandra Rose Hughes is a mother to five gorgeous image-bearers and two surly cats. A former high school English teacher, she is now a stay-at-home mom and writer. Her work has appeared in *Guideposts Magazine, The California Quarterly*, and will soon appear in the poetry anthology, *I've Got a Bad Case of Poetry*. Her work is also available in her personal poetry collection, *Why Faeries Bite*.

Sara Kay Mooney is a writer based in East Charlotte, where she lives with her husband and three children. Her work has been featured in *The Charlotte Observer, Bustle, Christianity Today*, and *Earth & Altar*, among other publications. A trained librarian, she currently helps manage communications at a global nonprofit. Follow her on Instagram (@skmreadspoetry) for her latest poetry recommendations.

Sara Luchuk grew up in South Jersey, where she discovered a love for forests and words. She went to college in East Tennessee, where she discovered a love for the Living Word (the True Vine). After college, she married Alan, and together they homeschooled three sons, seeking to share with them that love for forests, words, and the Living Word. Near the end of their homeschooling journey, the family moved to North Georgia, where Sara spent a few years sharing her love of forests, words, and the Living Word in a local library. Currently, the Living Word has moved her to focus her words on a chapter book for early elementary children. Through all these seasons and settings, poetry has bubbled to the surface. In all her writing, Sara seeks to paint pictures that point to the True Vine who is the source of every true word.

Sarah Elizabeth is a singer, musician, teacher, and writer living in Kansas City. She loves taking her dog Bella for walks, spinning donuts in the car on a snowy day, and searching for the best chai latte in KC. You can find her on Substack at wordsbysarahelizabeth.substack.com and Instagram @wordsbysarahelizabeth.

Sarah K. Butterfield, author of "Around the Clock Mom," is a writer, speaker, and ministry leader with a heart for empowering busy women to grow deeper in their faith and be intentional with their time. As part of this mission, Sarah hosts the *Theology on Purpose* podcast, as well as writes regularly for her own website (sarahkbutterfield.com). She and her husband and two boys live in sunny San Diego.

Sarah Lehman lives in rural Indiana where she enjoys creating through word, music, and art.

Sharon Rhyne is an author, gardener, wife, and Mother. She writes on faith, gardening, and grief at https://www.substack.com/@epiphanyofmystery.

Stacia Priscilla (Blank Stace) is a wife and a mother of two. She lives in Jakarta with her husband and daughters. Her poems have appeared in *Ekstasis Magazine, The Clayjar Review*, among others.

Taylor Blayse is a wife, writer, and greenhouse manager for her family's business, The Garden Party. She holds a B.A. in both music and English from the University of Missouri. In her writing, Taylor loves to explore themes of hope, whimsy, wonder, and childlike faith. Her writing has been published at *The Way Back to Ourselves, Humana Obscura, Twenty Hills, Prosetrics*, and others. When she isn't writing, she can be found reading, spending time with friends, gardening, wandering around bookstores, and enjoying the outdoors. To read more of her poetry and fiction, visit her substack or instagram: @taylorblayse.

Theresa Miller resides in the wide-open spaces of Wyoming, nestled near the Big Horn Mountains with her husband and four children. Weaving words has been her creative outlet since childhood, bringing clarity to life's complexities. Theresa is the co-author of *Unexpected Blessings: 40 Days of Discovering God's Best* and author of the Bible study, *The Posture of Victory: Finding True Peace amidst Our Everyday Battles*. When not writing, you can find Theresa cheering for her children's athletic events, running down a mountain, or jumping out of a plane. Learn more about her at www.theresammiller.com and on Instagram @theresammillerauthor.

Tonia Gütting combines a deep passion for Jesus with a love of writing, and she delights in discovering God's gifts, surrounded as she is on their little farm. Wonder is her favorite topic, and she is working on a book on it. Tonia loves to play, wrestle, work, and dance with words. She currently writes for military families for American Bible Society's HeroSquad program. Tonia and her retired Army Chaplain husband homeschooled their three children, who are now grown. On the farm, they play St. Francis to a couple of crazy pups, a small menagerie herd, and a grumpy cat. Tonia enjoys writing, teaching and speaking, reading and ruminating over a good cup of tea, as well as hiking and all things outdoors. She can be found at: https://toniagutting.com/author/tgutting/ and on Substack.

Zane Paxton is an emerging poet whose words seek to articulate the abundant life. His work has been featured by *Ekstasis*. He resides in Lincoln, NE with his wife and daughter. Connect and read more of his poems at https://zanepaxton.substack.com.